Raising teenagers

Raising teenagers

52 brilliant ideas for
high-performance parenting

Lynn Huggins-Cooper

brilliant
ideas

CAREFUL NOW

The information in this book should not be used instead of the advice and guidance given by professionals – but it will help you to navigate the dangerous swamp we call the teenage years. Consult your family health practitioner if you are at all concerned about your child's health or wellbeing as he/she acts as a gatekeeper for many services and can refer you on. Enquiring minds are good, and there are plenty of great organizations out there ready to help you and your teen – but don't be afraid to seek professional advice.

Although the contents of this book were checked at the time of going to press, the World Wide Web is constantly changing. This means the publisher and author cannot guarantee the contents of any of the websites mentioned in the text.

Copyright © The Infinite Ideas Company Limited, 2006

The right of Lynn Huggins-Cooper to be identified as the author of this book has been asserted in accordance with the Copyright, Designs and Patents Act 1988

First published in 2006 by
The Infinite Ideas Company Limited
36 St Giles
Oxford, OX1 3LD
United Kingdom
www.infideas.com

A CIP catalogue record for this book is available from the British Library

ISBN 1-904902-38-3

Brand and product names are trademarks or registered trademarks of their respective owners.

Designed by Baseline Arts Ltd, Oxford
Typeset by Sparks, Oxford
Printed by TJ International, Cornwall

Brilliant ideas

Brilliant features

Each chapter of this book is designed to provide you with an inspirational idea that you can read quickly and put into practice straight away.

Throughout you'll find four features that will help you get right to the heart of the idea:

- *Here's an idea for you ...* Take it on board and give it a go – right here, right now. Get an idea of how well you're doing so far.

- *Try another idea ...* If this idea looks like a life-changer then there's no time to lose. *Try another idea ...* will point you straight to a related tip to enhance and expand on the first.

- *Defining idea ...* Words of wisdom from masters and mistresses of the art, plus some interesting hangers-on.

- *How did it go?* If at first you do succeed, try to hide your amazement. If, on the other hand, you don't, then this is where you'll find a Q and A that highlights common problems and how to get over them.

Introduction

If you are living in a house with a child on the cusp of becoming a teenager, congratulations. I'm not being sarcastic; you are about to embark on an amazing voyage. It may be a bumpy ride, but on the journey your child will grow, change and blossom into the adult she will one day become. If you are living with an older teenager, I won't try to sugar coat it:
you will meet challenges. The raging hormones; the pressures of exams; the angst of relationships with friends and eventually lovers – modern teenagers are under so much pressure, it's no wonder they get moody!

Living with teens can be difficult because your child is in the process of great change. Gone is the baby who adored you without question; only shadows remain of the child who hung on your every word of wisdom. Your teenager is becoming a young adult, trying to find his way in the world. He is now programmed to reject your values and kick against your authority. Hence the piles of stinky laundry, festering around his room – he'll bring it down when he needs it, right? His penchant for alcopops and death metal is just a natural rejection of your middle aged, middle class values – OK? His refusal to go on outings with the family is natural – you are just too embarrassing. Get used to it.

Some days, when arguments are raging, music is blaring, dishes pile up in the sink and your daughter misses her curfew *again,* you may feel that you just can't bear it any longer.

But if you take a step backwards, breathing deeply for a moment, you will be able to see that most of the problems and irritations we have when parenting teens are small ones. It's only because we are so close to them that they look so big. It's all about perspective.

That's not to say that parenting teens is easy. Your 'baby' is metamorphosing into the adult he or she will be, and it's hard to watch. You want to save them from making your mistakes, and make their lives easier. Newsflash: you can't.

What you can – and must – do is always be there to listen. There will be times when you are the last person she wants to talk to, but you must make sure the opportunity is always there. Be available. It is too easy to get caught up in the whirl of work and other commitments and to forget that your child – however adult she may wish to appear – still needs you, and your guidance. Research shows that teenagers who have stronger relationships with their parents are less likely to end up in *serious* trouble. It's not rocket science: it's common sense. The hard thing is maintaining the strong relationship you built when she was a child, without trying to stifle her. It's not always easy, but it is possible.

Your teenager is living in difficult times. It seems that there are temptations at every turn and the newspapers are full of under-age binge drinking, drug abuse and teen sexual experimentation. Exam stress is at an all time high. Many teens are suffering from depression, eating disorders and low self esteem. Added to that, young people are in a unique position where society – including parents – expects them to act in a responsible fashion, yet gives them few real choices or autonomy. It is hard to be a modern teenager!

Hold on to the fact that you laid good foundations in your teenager's childhood as his character was forming and he was more impressionable. The framework of guidance you gave him then will continue to help him now.

Try to remember what *you* were like when you were a teenager. Just like your child, you experimented and made mistakes on your way to finding out exactly who you are. Remembering this will help you to recognise some of the problems your teen faces.

This book will help you to consider the pressures your teen is under, and give you ideas about how to cope, and where to seek further help if necessary. Above all, remember that there is no such thing as a perfect parent. All parents shout, say things they regret, and mess up. You are a human being, so be kind to yourself rather than judgemental. Expend your energy instead on making efforts to connect with your teenager. Spend time together, just hanging out. The best and most intimate of conversations often happen over a TV show and a snack! Whatever happens, believe in them, especially if they are struggling. Don't weigh them down with your expectations – they have enough baggage of their own. Remember, if it's hard parenting a teen, it's even harder to be one.

Lynn Huggins-Cooper

1

All change here for the puberty express!

Puberty creeps up on children and performs magic tricks on them overnight. Your baby is in the process of metamorphosing into the adult that he will become.

These changes can hit unwary parents like an express train, so read on to be prepared!

Adolescence and puberty can be a challenging time, characterised by massive change which is not just physical, but also emotional and behavioural. Teenagers often feel self-conscious about their bodies, and unsure of themselves. They are taking their first shaky steps towards independent adult life – and, behind the bluster, they are scared. They may become over reliant on friends of the same age, and they may feel the need to become part of a group – dressing the same, wearing the same make up, listening to the same music etc. – which makes them feel more secure. Go with the flow – if it makes them feel better, and hurts no one, what's the harm in a *penchant* for black/uber-fashion/studs/long hair/super short hair/deathly pallor make up (delete as applicable)?

As your child goes through puberty, her skin will produce an increased amount of an oily substance called sebum. It can make hair and skin greasy and blackheads and spots can develop. The hormonal surge can also cause an increase in sweat – and body odour. Make sure you provide your child with a range of toiletries to cope with these changes. Make it casual, but provide her with a box of her own goodies such as deodorant, medicated skin wash and cleanser. Top it up on a regular basis.

They still need you and the guidance you offer – even if they think they don't. The arguments you have are only a natural expression of their efforts to pull away from you and the ties that they see as binding them to childhood.

Try to remember at all times that adolescence can be a miserable, lonely time – even for the most outwardly 'popular' kids. Adolescents are daily rocked by a maelstrom of feelings and emotions, but often the last thing they want to do is talk to you about it. Develop a hard carapace and don't take it personally! All parents, including counsellors, psychologists and parenting 'experts,' have problems communicating with their teenagers. Trust me: I know *that* fact at first hand.

Dealing with all the changes they experience can leave your child tired, clumsy and moody. He may sleep more – it can feel as though the faeries have stolen away your lively, delightful child in the night, only to leave an unresponsive, teenager-shaped lump inhabiting your house in his stead!

WHAT DOES *PUBERTY* MEAN IN PHYSICAL TERMS?

Puberty is the process of changing from a child to an adult, capable (at least in *physical* terms) of sexual reproduction. It usually begins between eight and thirteen in girls and ten and fifteen in boys, but there can be wide variation within this period.

IT'S A GIRL THING

Usually a girl's breasts start to develop first. Breast buds – small lumps behind the nipples – start to grow and then expand. Sometimes breasts develop unevenly so one is bigger than the other – assure your daughter that they will even out more as they grow, and that most women have some slight variation in breast size.

Next, pubic hair begins to grow, followed by underarm hair. She will find an increase in clear or white discharge on her pants, which is totally normal as her body prepares for her periods to start.

Be aware that girls who develop early can feel very self-conscious. Buy her a bra as soon as she wants or needs one. If she rejects a bra at first, compromise with a crop top. I have fond memories of my first bra, needed at age ten, with a great picture of the cartoon character 'Top Cat' on each boob. Hunt around and let your daughter choose her own new undies. At this age most kids still don't want to feel 'different' – but that, like all things, will pass!

BOYS WILL BE BOYS

The first sign of puberty in most boys is an increase in the size of the testicles and penis. They generally find *this* sign pretty exciting! Reassure him that any difference he notices in penis size between him and his mates is only noticeable in the non erect penis – and most

Try another idea…

Is your teen having problems with pimples? Look at IDEA 42, *Let's face it – acne anxieties*, for a few tips on dealing with acne.

Defining idea…

'*You don't have to suffer to be a poet; adolescence is enough suffering for anyone.*'
ARTHUR C. COXE, bishop and writer of hymns

penises are of a similar size once erect. On the subject of penises, let him know that embarrassing, badly timed erections are a fact of life – they don't make him a sex maniac! Just give him strategies to cope, such as thinking about other things etc.

Pubic and underarm hair also starts to sprout, and his voice deepens. His muscles will grow, as will his appetite – stand by for the fridge to empty itself overnight on a regular basis – and he will shoot up in height. Sometimes boys can look gangly before they 'grow into' their new size and lay down muscle. Lastly, he will develop wispy facial hair.

How did it go?

Q   When should I expect my daughter to start her periods?

A   Periods are usually (but not always) the last 'puberty' development to appear. She may be as young as nine or as old as fifteen, with girls averaging menarche (first period) at around 12½ – it varies enormously. Periods are delayed in thinner girls, not usually starting until weight reaches at least 45kg.

Q   My son is 14, and upset that he looks much younger than his friends. How can I reassure him?

A   Your son will develop when his own biological clock tells him he is ready. Tell him he will catch up soon – he may not seem to believe you, but he needs to hear it. Tell him about the website: http://www.teengrowth.com – he should find it reassuring.

2

Stranger than fiction ...

The word 'teenager' describes any young person between the ages of thirteen and nineteen, but the media seems to see teens as some strange, alien, disaffected antisocial group.

These stereotypes are not just stupid and ill informed; they are harmful. Moral panics about teenagers create a divide of 'them' and 'us' in society.

The last thing your daughter needs is to feel any more alienated from society – and more specifically from you, as her parent. The negative images of teenagers in the media can help to drive a wedge between generations, but sensationalism sells. If you buy in to these stereotypes, you are in danger of demonising your daughter's friends and peers, and that will only distance her from your care.

A recent survey found that more than half (54%) of teenagers questioned believe they have a poor reputation in their community. Only 13% felt that society values them. An amazing 19% felt that 'bad press' and being stereotyped was the worst thing about being a teenager. That made it a greater concern for teens than exam pressures, mood swings and relationship problems.

Your daughter and her peers need your support and understanding, not hostility. You and I built the society our teenagers live in; we need to equip them with the tools to survive inside it, rather than blame them for society's problems.

MEDIA MYTHS: 'TEENAGE SEX'

The media is full of headlines trumpeting the irresponsibility of teenagers having unprotected sex, and ghoulish stories of sexual health clinics full of diseased or pregnant teens abound. Teenagers are portrayed as too immature to have safe sex, only 'indulging' as a result of peer pressure. Calls are made for abstinence, and references are made to 'the good old days' when teenagers waited until they were married.

Here's an idea for you...

Make sure your son knows that you do not subscribe to the negative view of teenagers promoted in the media. Discuss the issues raised in media reports with your child, and keep channels of communication open. Make sure they 'overhear' you praising actions taken by young people in society. Do not let a 'them and us' culture develop in your family.

Of course, the reality is somewhat different. Teenagers have always had sex. In the 1980s, the parents of today's teens were at it; there was an explosion of sexually transmitted diseases and AIDS reared its ugly head. In the 1960s and 70s, free love ruled – and that included the teenage community. In the 1940s, teens (like the rest of society) had sex to prove they were alive – and in case that suddenly changed. So it goes on, into the past. But a moral dilemma is whipped up in the media about 'immoral' teens and a myth is perpetuated.

If you buy into – and sound off about – the idea that 'MTV culture' is encouraging teens to have sex you risk alienating your teen, so she does not want to talk to you about sex because of the danger that you will lecture her, or be shocked.

MEDIA MYTHS: 'TEENAGE VIOLENCE'

The media is full of images of lawless teens left to roam the streets with a slap on the wrist. Crime figures tell a different story. In the US, for every violent and sexual offence committed by an under 18, there are three such crimes committed by adults against children and teens. The myth of violent teens is a smokescreen, in which politicians condemn the behaviour and moral values of teenagers, knowing it is a guaranteed crowd-pleaser (the problems are with *them*; not us). Sensational stories of 'granny-bashing teens on the rampage' sell papers. Once again, if you believe the moral panic, you are condemning your own child – she is a teen too. You may believe that these terrible teens live somewhere 'out there' – you don't believe they have anything to do with your daughter and her friends – but if you voice your concerns that teens are wild and violent as the media portrays them, you will lose credibility with your daughter, and that will widen the distance between you.

Worried about the dangers of labelling your teen? Read IDEA 47, *Labelling is disabling – giving your teen a bad name*, for ideas on how to avoid the trap.

Try another idea...

'Like its politicians and its wars, society has the teenagers it deserves.'
J. B. PRIESTLEY, author

Defining idea...

How did it go?

Q   **I know teens can look scary, all sat in a group in the centre of town, but I get fed up of hearing people moan about them. My son meets his friends on a Saturday afternoon to chat – not cause trouble. My husband is worried that he will get into trouble, as we already know that the police are not keen on these gatherings, and move the kids on. What can I do?**

A   *Teens have always liked to get together – they are probably not plotting the downfall of society; they are more likely to be discussing music and fashion, and moaning about their curfews! Make sure your son has somewhere to bring his friends, undisturbed, if he wants to. His bedroom should be a good place for them to gather – add seating, cushions, maybe a kettle and cups. But reassure your husband that this 'flocking' behaviour is an entirely normal phase which your son will outgrow. Have a word with your son to let him know his friends are welcome – and that you will keep out of the way!*

Q   **I'm fed up with signs in shops that say 'only two schoolchildren at a time' and the general view that all teens need watching constantly or they will get up to something. I want to reassure my son about this, but I'm a bit worried about sounding like some sort of 'cool mum' wannabe – how can I avoid this?**

A   *Well, don't launch into some dreadful 'I'm down with the kids' monologue, reminiscent of a sad old radio DJ who's past his sell-by date! Instead, discuss with your son why people may have a dim view of teens when you see an example in the media or you hear someone making disparaging comments. It is a prejudice like any other and should be challenged.*

3

Too much pressure

Many teenagers come back from school to an empty house; and when their parents do get back they are often tired and preoccupied. So, how can you make sure you still make time to connect?

Families have changed shape in recent decades. The average family today is likely to have both parents out at work, with young children in nursery or childminder care; school aged children are cared for in after school clubs or other types of childcare — possibly with grandparents.

Many children are being brought up by single parents – mostly single through relationship breakdown, divorce or bereavement. The number of families headed by lone parents has more than trebled in the past 25 years, accounting for 20% of all families with children. This can increase the pressure on the family as one parent is burdened with all the mundane, day-to-day tasks that make up family life, with no partner to share the load. If your extended family lives far away, and is unable to help, this only increases the difficulties.

As support networks shrink, the issues we face as parents can seem to loom larger. When it comes to parenting teenagers, the task can be so complex and delicate – and just plain baffling – that we need people to lean on. As you become more 'absent' from family life, due to the pressures of work, your teenager will miss your influence – even if he thinks quite the opposite! He needs you there as a role model, but even more, he needs you there as a sounding board. Can you arrange to work from home maybe once or twice a week? He may have nothing major about school to 'report', but the small hurts of everyday life such as snubs from other kids, sarcastic teachers, worries about school work or issues about self image can be soothed in a low key, nurturing manner by a parent or carer present at the right time. It's amazing what can be sorted out over a hot chocolate and a biscuit!

Here's an idea for you…

Try to make at least one 'date' with your teenager each week, even if it's just a girly shopping trip or a quick pizza. If you can't be there when she comes home from school, try to eat together as a family round the table at least a couple of times a week for shared time when everyone can catch up.

Much is said – on talk shows; in magazine articles and interviews – about the importance of spending 'quality time' with your children. This is true even more where teeenagers are concerned. If you want your teenager to make time for you, you must make time for him. Not a regular heart to heart session – he is likely to recoil in horror at the very thought of such a scenario. Rather, make sure you share things together – go to gigs together, enjoy a sporting activity or show, or go to see a film. In our house, cooking a meal together is a good time for 'casual but important' conversations. You will need to find what works for you.

If you are not around, your child will turn to someone else. Whilst it is normal for teenagers to consult their peers on everything from style issues to views on the world, they also need input from mature, more worldly-wise mentors. A mentor, or significant adult, can help your teenager to make wise choices when it comes to big issues such as sex, drugs and alcohol. For your own piece of mind, you want to be in a position to be that significant adult. If you are not around or available, your teenager will turn solely to his peers, and the advice they give may not be what you are hoping for. When teens are not actually ensconced with their friends, they are permanently attached via email, text, phone or instant messenger. If you are not around to temper the views of their peers – which may or may not be sensible – these are the views they will internalize.

Concerned that your teen may be becoming depressed? See IDEA 51, *Nobody understands me*, for ideas on how to cope.

Try another idea…

In a recent study of 12,000 teenagers and their parents, researchers found that the single most important predictor of the wellbeing of the teenagers studied was their relationship with their parents, regardless of family type. The study included teenagers with two parents of the same and different sexes, and teenagers in lone parent households. The basic message is, your child still needs you – perhaps more than ever!

'Nobody has ever before asked the nuclear family to live all by itself in a box the way we do. With no relatives, no support, we've put it in an impossible situation.'
MARGARET MEAD, anthropologist

Defining idea…

How did it go?

Q   I am in the process of getting a divorce. How can I make things easier for my teenager?

A   *Make sure your teenager knows you will still be Mum and Dad even though you are not a couple any more. Although they seem mature, do not burden her with details and your feelings – find another shoulder to cry on. Your teenager will need support from you, in dealing with her own feelings. Be aware that teens tend to see things in terms of black and white, and make sure there are no 'good guys' and 'villains' in the proceedings. If you set a good example for managing conflict, you will give your teen an invaluable life lesson.*

Q   I try to talk to my teen but she just grunts at me and makes it clear she does not want to talk. What can I do to open a dialogue?

A   *You will need to work at it. Make sure that you don't fall into the trap of moaning at your teen every time you speak to her! Don't try to launch straight into 'big issues' – general chat is a good starting point. Find something she is interested in (music, sport – whatever) and start with a few comments about that. And don't try too hard – it will show. Going out for some kind of shared activity, such as a trip to the cinema might help – you can at least talk about the film! Eventually she will talk to you!*

4

Letting go: the sharpest learning curve

Parenting teens requires a whole new set of skills, over and above the parenting skills you have learned as your child has grown from baby to toddler, and toddler to child. The hardest of these is learning to let go.

You will make mistakes, but be kind to yourself — you are new at this!

The hardest thing to accept as your child grows up is that you do not have that much control over another person's life. Although you want to shelter your teenager from the harm and hurts that life can bring, the reality is that she needs to make mistakes just as you did. This is an incredibly hard lesson to learn.

Accepting this fact is like going into free fall. It makes your stomach churn. Your child is moving away from you – and that's natural and proper. No longer do you know precisely what they are doing and exactly who they are with every moment of the day as you did when she was smaller. You can't sugar coat this – it's awful.

Here's an idea for you...

Play the 'what if ...?' game with your teenager. It is a continuation of the 'what would you do if you were lost in a shop?' type game you play with younger children. Rehearse with your child what they would do in a variety of scenarios. What if ... people were drinking and they didn't want to? If a friend supposed to give them a lift somewhere was drinking and driving? If he felt threatened at a party? Tailor the scenarios to your child's age and situation. The bottom line is, he needs to know you or another trusted adult will go and collect him in an emergency.

Younger teens especially still need to keep in close contact with you (thank god for mobile phones!) to let you know where they are and when they will return. They may chafe against this, but as they make the transition from child to teen they need to understand that there are dangers in the world outside their home environment. The dangers only continue – and even multiply – as your child gets older and starts going out to pubs and clubs. My middle daughter used to roll her eyes as I read the latest horror out of the newspaper about abductions and date rape – it got to be a family joke. The point was made, however, and allowed me to talk with her about my fears. Interestingly enough, she can now be heard passing on similar advice and concern to her younger sister …

There are things you can do though to reassure yourself, and to keep your child as safe as possible.

- Keep a telephone list of your child's friends' home and mobile numbers. The mobile numbers help when you are trying to contact your child and she has forgotten it/has it turned off/run out of charge.
- Remember what it was like to be a teenager. You were one once! That doesn't mean embarrassing your daughter with horrific stories about the 'high jinks'

you used to get up to. Rather, try to remember the desire to be treated as a grown up; the need for privacy and the need to be permanently grafted to the phone to check out what your friends are doing/wearing/thinking.

If your teen is going out alone in the evenings, read IDEA 48, *Safe as houses – teaching your teen about personal safety*, for tips on personal safety.

Try another idea...

- Be aware that you will not *necessarily* share views or standards of behaviour with the parents of your child's friends. It can come as a nasty shock to find that other parents are much more lenient in areas such as alcohol use, smoking dope, teenage sexual behaviour etc. It is worth carrying out some gentle probing here to explore views before your child gets into a habit of staying over for impromptu parties etc. This conversation should be non-confrontational – perhaps share your worries about (unspecified) friends shehas made who are allowed greater freedom and test the water that way. Do not be tempted to ask her, however – it is a generally accepted rule (according to teenagers) that everybody else has more freedom than they have and you are a prehistoric throwback/don't trust them/want to make them look stupid – so you may as well get used to it.
- Set ground rules about staying in touch; tailored to your teenager's age and maturity. Let her know that you can't help worrying, but she can put your mind at rest – and so keep you off her back – with a phone call or text message to let you know if her arrangements change or she has missed the bus etc.

Having teenagers can be nerve wracking, but try to develop an optimistic outlook, hard though that can be! That way you will make sure you don't allow your anxiety to sabotage your relationship with your teen.

'Having children makes you no more a parent than having a piano makes you a pianist.'
MICHAEL LEVINE

Defining idea...

15

How did it go?

Q **My 17 year old is very secretive about where he goes and what he does. I don't think he gets up to anything awful, but I would sleep easier at night if I knew a little more about his friends. He used to have people round all the time, but that happens rarely these days. What can I do?**

A *Make it clear to your son that his friends are welcome – suggest he invites them round to listen to music/study/play computer games, making it clear you will provide pizza and snacks but won't hang around and embarrass him! He may feel that you would rather not have groups of his mates hanging around.*

Q **My son has a mobile phone but objects to calling me to let me know where he is because it costs him money. Am I being unreasonable?**

A *Not about wanting to know where he is – but in our house we give our teens small amounts of money to top up their phones on a regular basis (they also top up their phones themselves) with the understanding that they will always have money left for emergencies.*

5

Why are they so weird?

Teenagers sometimes seem like a different species – but there's a reason for that!

Newsflash — their brains are actually different to ours — so they can't help it!

Parents are not the only ones to puzzle about the workings of the teenage brain. Scientists have used advanced scanning methods to study the chemical and structural changes that occur in the brains of adolescents. They have found that the brain continues to grow and change past childhood and well into the teenage period of development.

Teenagers take risks   all parents of teenagers know this. But scientists have discovered a reason why this is the case. They have found that the emotional region of the brain develops to maturity way before the area of the brain that is responsible for rational thought.

Here's something the frazzled parents of teens could have told the scientists without the need for expensive research: teenagers have heightened emotions but have not yet acquired the ability to think things through carefully. At least now we have scientific proof …

Here's an idea for you...
Offer your teen safe thrills! She will crave the excitement that risk taking brings, so help her to get it out of her system in a safe environment.
Encourage her to take part in exciting, physically challenging pursuits such as scuba diving, abseiling, rock climbing, snowboarding, kayaking, surfing and caving. This will allow her to explore her wild side in a safety controlled environment.

When your son acts on impulse, and takes part in risky behaviour, it may not be his raging hormones, but his brain development that's to blame. He takes more risks than you because he is unable to consider the outcomes and consequences of his actions in the same way as you would. His frontal lobes – the part of the brain responsible for logic, anticipating consequences, planning and organisation – are not mature, and won't be until he is around 25. That means that even the most sensible teen can make very bad decisions in a moment of excitement, usually experienced in a group of friends – so he will make mistakes.

Of course, the added complication is that your son's brain is in turmoil at the same time as he has access to 'new toys' such as cars, alcohol, cigarettes, and even drugs. Obviously, any mind or mood altering substances can exacerbate the problem, encouraging 'wild' behaviour as inhibitions are discarded. It can make for a lot of sleepless nights …

HOW TO COPE

Be there

Stay in close contact with his world. Make sure you have lots of no-conflict time together where you are just hanging around together. It makes it more likely that they will run things by you (even in a scandalised tone) to get your take on things that other teens have done. You can give them a valuable extra opinion.

Talk about the consequences of risky behaviour

Talk about what happens when teens take part in risky behaviour – perhaps when you are reading the paper and appropriate stories present themselves. My kids groan as I read some horror story about teen drink driving, but the message drip feeds into their consciousness. Be ready to talk about actual examples of kids you know if your son or daughter comes home and tells you about a peer who is pregnant, or has gotten into trouble with the police etc. Your teen can use the discussions as a 'what if…?' experiment, and you can even role-play different scenarios to carry out a risk assessment of certain activities and situations.

Does your teenage child's risky behaviour make you concerned about alcohol? Check out IDEA 19, *The demon drink: your teen and alcohol*, for ways to deal with the problem.

Try another idea…

'I don't know why I did it, I don't know why I enjoyed it, and I don't know why I'll do it again.'

SOCRATES

Defining idea…

19

Questions to ask your teen about risk taking:

■ Do you feel pressured by friends to make risky choices? How can you avoid that pressure?

■ Do you rush into making important decisions, or do you discuss things with trusted friends?

■ Do dangerous risks feel exciting? What other activities make you feel the same buzz?

■ Do you make dangerous choices to show off to other people? Does it give you status with your friends?

Remember, this is not an interrogation! Be prepared to talk about and examine your own behaviours and motivations to create a 'sharing' atmosphere.

Appeal to their vanity

Point out research findings to your kids. Psychologists think that teens have an inbuilt attitude that bad things happen to other people. This trait is called *cognitive egocentrism*. If you warn your teen about most dangers – from alcohol poisoning to sexually transmitted diseases – he is quite likely to reassure you that he knows these terrible things happen – but it won't happen to him. Your teen thinks he is invulnerable, and he's going to live forever. Why not try a cunning tack to break through their veneer of confidence: appeal to his vanity. Let him know that smoking causes extreme wrinkling; that over consumption of alcohol can cause dry, brittle hair and even hair loss; that taking amphetamines or Ecstasy potentially causes 'speed willy' – a shrunken penis. These ideas resonate long after your warnings about risky behaviour.

Q   **Is all risk taking harmful then? I worry that if my daughter takes no risks and is constantly protected that she will not be able to look after herself.**

How did it go?

A   *Risk taking is a vital tool that your daughter needs to learn to use to shape her life. If she never learns how to assess risks, she will never build a career or a serious relationship! It is only when the risk taking becomes dangerous that parents need to take action. Otherwise, just support and encourage her as she finds her way in the world – even if your heart is in your mouth!*

Q   **How do you talk risks through with your daughter without sounding like a prim educational video?**

A   *Try to be natural, and talk about things as they come up. A friend's teenage daughter got pregnant; we talked through consequences such as the mother having a severely curtailed social life because of taking the lion's share of care duties – and the impact on college. Both of my teens know that whatever they do they will still be loved and welcome in the family home (a point worth making), but they know that behaviour has consequences attached. Try the same with your teens.*

6

Parenting the pod person

Who stole your kid in the night? Sometimes it feels that way – the lovely little companion who happily went on outings with you disappears, to be replaced by someone too terminally cool to be involved in anything *you* enjoy!

Take heart; this stage too will soon pass.
Your daughter is an individual. Remember, she isn't
you, and doesn't want to be you.

Adolescence does not happen overnight, even though it sometimes feels that way. What happens in reality is that the changes have been taking place, but we suddenly notice. You are no longer the all powerful parent. These changes are incredibly hard to adjust to, but adjust we must.

The cardinal rule for parenting this strange new creature is this: Don't try to make her into something she is not. All you will do is cause frustration for yourself and resentment in your teenager. Don't mourn the child she was – remember her with affection. She is still in there somewhere, under the black eyeliner and hairspray!

Instead, work towards building a new relationship with your developing teenager. This will form the basis of your relationship with her, so it is worth working at. You must make sure you truly accept the new person your child is becoming. You may think this is a given – of course you accept her – you love her, warts and all. But does your behaviour or what you say give a different message?

If you get into a litany of criticism, correction and (the cardinal sin) comparison with another child, your teen may feel rejected. She may feel unloved, and that she has no value in your eyes. If she feels this, she is likely to act out her feelings of rejection and the cycle begins again. She is difficult; you react; she feels rejected and acts out her feelings of unloveliness.

Never compare one child to another. If you compare your daughter's behaviour, academic prowess – whatever – to a sibling, you may be hoping to motivate her, but all you are doing is making her feel angry and unworthy. You may even drive a wedge between siblings that could take decades to shift. Don't do it.

Here's an idea for you...

Avoid getting into a negative mindset with your teenage son. Think about how your parents made you feel about yourself when *you* were a teenager. Visualise yourself back in that situation. This will allow you to contextualise your son's attitude towards you, and may help you to manage your own behaviour.

Sometimes it is too easy to drone on about mistakes your daughter has made. Don't dwell on the past. Look firmly ahead and build a better future with her by focussing firmly on her good qualities – and accept that some days you will have to dig deep to find them!

Avoid using damaging labels such as *bad, stupid* or *lazy*. As when parenting younger children, remember to criticise the behaviour, not the person. Say 'That was rather unkind', rather than 'You are unkind'. Do not offer your child mental and emotional images of herself that are unhealthy and negative. She will be good enough at doing that all by herself.

CATCH HER BEING GOOD!

Struggling to remember what it was like to be a teenager? Look at Idea 7, *The still small voice: listening to your inner teenager*, and wallow in the memories!

Try another idea…

Take time every week to show your teenage child that you value her. Recognise and praise her talents, whatever they are. She may be creative, good at sport or very caring. Get the message across that no one can be talented in all areas – we are all different.

Watch out for the things your teenager loves to do, and encourage her. Be ready to give support to develop her aptitudes, even if that means spending money on sports kit or art supplies! This will encourage her to develop her talents. Be careful though that your child does not become labelled as 'the arty one' or 'the sporty one' as this can become restricting in itself, narrowing her boundaries.

It is natural to encourage qualities and talents that you value personally – perhaps because they mirror your own interests and talents, and you think it will be something you can share. Be careful, though. Remember, your teenager is not made in your image, and don't get carried away! Just because you enjoy something, it doesn't mean she will. Be patient about things your child finds difficult. Just because you are academic, it does not naturally follow that your daughter will be the top of her class. You may be a great dancer; she may be uncoordinated. Do not put her under pressure to live up to *your* standards.

'Nothing has a stronger influence psychologically on their environment and especially on their children than the unlived life of the parent.'

CARL JUNG, psychologist

Defining idea…

Look for and develop *her* natural talents and resist trying to develop the talents you think she should have. My eldest is a talented actor, and I can't act my way out of a paper bag. I can appreciate and foster his talent, however. My eldest daughter is a talented sportswoman. I have two left feet and can't catch – I'm so bad, it's a family joke. I can still celebrate and nurture her skills, though. You will enjoy supporting your child, and may even learn new skills yourself.

How did it go?

Q   **My teenager constantly compares himself to his friends who he sees as more popular, and more talented. How can I help him to be happier with who he is?**

A   *Praise, praise, and more praise – and hugs, if he lets you! Keep up a low level backing track of encouragement. Don't try to refute his statements about his friends; concentrate on building up his own sense of worth.*

Q   **My child seems to be more interested in being surly and awkward rather than displaying obvious talents! I want to encourage him – where can I start?**

A   *Think about what he was interested in as a child and start from there. If you find him critical and 'awkward', why not turn that into a positive and encourage him to develop skills in critical thinking, or to join a pressure group with views he feels passionate about, such as environmental issues, animal welfare or youth politics?*

7

The still small voice: listening to your inner teenager

Much has been written about the 'inner child.' If you are in touch with yours – congratulations. But your inner child has a taller, surlier sibling: your inner teenager.

To help you to connect with your own teenager, you need to get in touch with your inner teenager. This trip down memory lane will remind yourself of who you once were, in order to understand better exactly who your inner teenager is.

Ask yourself – 'Am I the person I thought I would be when I was a child?' The chances are you won't be – unless you are a pirate, princess, spaceman, or fire fighter! You can afford to smile indulgently at the child you once were, and his or her hopes and dreams.

Here's an idea for you... **Write a letter, as a parent, to your teenage self. List the great things about yourself, and be encouraged to let go of the things you felt bad about. You can find the roots of many destructive behaviour patterns in your teenage years, and giving yourself the validation you may not have received as a real teenager can help you to break those patterns. You can parent and nurture yourself. Welcoming and caring for your inner teenager can help you to connect with your own teenager, as you remember the challenges and insecurities of the teenage period.**

Ask yourself another question now – 'Does my life measure up to the expectations of adulthood I fostered when I was a teenager?' That's a more difficult question to answer, and demands honest soul searching to find the answer.

The chances are, you were an idealistic teenager. Most teenagers are. They live with a heightened sense of reality and believe they are going to reinvent the world; revolutionaries in thick eye make up and improbable clothing. As a radical teenage student at the LSE, I was permanently attached to a banner, protesting about everything from Maggie Thatcher's treatment of the miners to the banning of nuclear weapons. My preferred fashion was my dad's fireman jacket and skin tight, stripy red and black trousers. Nights were spent hotly debating politics in the Union bar or at the many 'benefit' concerts to raise money for the latest cause. It was a utopian existence, full of passion and excitement.

But life changes. A parent at 21, the rhythms of my life suddenly included breast-feeding, changing nappies and nurturing a new life. I was still an idealist; I still went along on protest marches, pushing a buggy – but my focus had changed.

The teenager I was never went away; she became preoccupied. As the years passed she became stifled under layers of responsibility – the children, the mortgage, the job.

Apart from occasional bouts of petulance, it wasn't until I had teenagers of my own that I remembered fully the girl I once was. The memories came back in waves. As you listen to your own teenager – his angst; his hopes and dreams; his hurts and challenges – remember the person you once were. It doesn't even matter if you are a different gender to your teenager; the experiences you had and the tender and confused feelings they created can be invaluable.

Teenage angst has become so often discussed that it is almost a cliché. But stop for a moment and try to recall how it felt to be so insecure about your appearance that a spot before an important date felt like the end of the world. This will help you to avoid the trap of trivialising your teenager's problems. It is too easy to be dismissive of his very real concerns when you are worried about meeting the mortgage payments, or caring for your elderly parents.

Try to remember the pressure you felt under to do well at school, to 'be somebody.' Remember the 'pep talks' you used to get from your parents and teachers about all the potential you had and what a sin it would be to waste it. Multiply that about ten times and that will be close to how your teen feels. Don't believe the hype that exams are easier today. If you don't believe me, buy a few sample papers. Try to remember how you felt as you waited for your results, feeling that your future depended on them.

If listening to your inner teenager has reminded you of the stresses teens are under, read IDEA 50, *Distress or de-stress?*, for ways to alleviate the strain.

Try another idea…

'We are the people our parents warned us about.'
JIMMY BUFFETT

Defining idea…

If you remember even a little of the tension, you will be able to cut your teenager some slack as he bites your head off when you ask him how his exam went ...

How did it go?

Q **Everything is so 'black and white' to my teenager. Things are either totally cool or below distain. How can I help her to be more mature, and see the middle ground in anything?**

A *Firstly, accept that you can't! Teenagers are programmed to act in this way. Perhaps it is because they are making so many decisions about the world and their place in it that they have to see things in simplified terms in order to cope. All you can do is to keep chipping away, trying to introduce balance and perspective. It may feel as though you are spitting into the wind, but eventually your teenager will mellow and remember the things you once said.*

Q **My teenage son is afraid to ask girls out. I find that weird because I was always popular with the girls. What can I do to help him?**

A *Firstly, remember the mantra: he is not you, and doesn't want to be you. Secondly, are you sure you aren't wearing rose tinted glasses? You were probably rejected plenty of times – so think hard and be honest with yourself. You are in danger of passing on your views to your son and making him feel even worse. Your son is afraid of rejection – as we all are. He feels conspicuous and insecure. Help him by trying to persuade him that even if he is rejected sometimes, it is not a comment on his value as a person – it's just a case of the wrong girl or the wrong time.*

8

Learning to listen: how to open channels of communication

What turns a chatty child, who delights in telling you all about her day, into the unresponsive lump that shrugs her shoulders and grunts 'Nothing' when asked about school, and accuses you of nagging at every turn?

She's not just being awkward. She's finding life confusing, and perhaps it's just easier to keep things to herself. But communication is the key to relationships, and you need to keep channels open so you can you offer your daughter the support she needs.

As humans, we communicate the whole time. Gestures, facial expressions, body language and eye contact all speak as loudly as our words. We should be experts, but communicating with our own teenagers can be a minefield.

Here's an idea for you... **Make sure you make time to give your son full attention when he is talking to you. Stop what you are doing, turn towards him and look at his face. Do not just carry on with whatever task you are doing. Turn towards him and be an 'active' listener – actually engage with what he says. This gives him the message that what he says – and by implication, he himself – is important to you.**

Firstly, we need to accept that this is part of their quest for freedom. They are changing into adults, and are trying to develop their own picture of the world and their place in it. Whilst you are crucial to this process, you must accept their view of you as having a 'supporting role' at best! It can be hard, when you have been at the centre of your child's life, to suddenly find yourself marginalised, but during the teenage years, your child needs you to listen twice as much as talk. She will use you as a sounding board, sometimes making crass pronouncements seemingly designed to shock you. Actually, she is testing you out – not in a calculated sense, but rather she is checking that she is 'safe' – she can talk to you about anything without fear of being judged. Despite the bravado and the protestations, our teenage children still need our support and understanding.

BUILDING A 'LISTENING' HOME

There are steps you can take to make it easier to communicate with your teenager. Try them out, and minimise the door slamming, tears and sulking (and that's just you!).

- Perhaps, most importantly, you must deal with your own hang-ups. Work through the things that make you feel awkward, discussing them with your partner or a close friend. This could mean sex and contraception, relationships, feelings, or risky behaviour. Once you feel more comfortable discussing these things generally, you will be better equipped to discuss them comfortably with your teenager, with an open mind.

If you are finding it hard to make time to communicate with your teenager, check out IDEA 14, *Making time*, for tips.

Try another idea…

- Try to see your daughter's point of view, and try to remember how passionately you felt about things at her age. But don't be afraid to share your views too. Avoid the cardinal sin of trying to bend your views to be trendy; she will see through your efforts and find it all a bit 'sad'. Be flexible, but remain true to yourself.

- Be positive. It's easy when you feel defeated by your daughter's attitude to fall into a negative mindset where you are constantly critical. Instead of saying, 'You make this house look like a tip, leaving your things everywhere,' say 'Please tidy your things away'. You may need to repeat this one …

- Offer genuine praise when your daughter has made efforts to be helpful or has modified her behaviour in response to a request from you. When you praise her, do not add a qualifying (and negating) 'but' at the end. In other words, don't say 'I'm glad you tidied up your room, but you have left loads of towels on the floor in the bathroom and you didn't rinse the bath …' etc., etc. Keep it separate.

- Don't routinely lecture your daughter, thinking you must always know best. Treat her ideas (and thus her) with respect. Listen carefully – you might learn something!

'Feelings of worth can flourish only in an atmosphere where individual differences are appreciated, mistakes are tolerated, communication is open, and rules are flexible – the kind of atmosphere that is found in a nurturing family.'
VIRGINIA SATIR

Defining idea…

■ Choose your battles. Don't expend great efforts trying to make your teenage child try to accept your point of view if it is not an important issue; save your efforts for important decisions she is less likely to see you as irritating background noise.

How did it go?

Q **My son shies away from talking to me about important issues, such as sex and alcohol. Actually, he doesn't seem to want to talk to me about much at all. What can I do to improve matters?**

A *Make sure you are making enough opportunities for 'casual talk' – do not just launch in, expecting a discussion about delicate issues! Suggest going out for a coffee or a shopping trip regularly just to get used to each other's 'chat' again in a relaxed setting. Don't try to force him to talk to you about complex and intimate issues; you have to earn his trust first.*

Q **My teenager says I don't listen to him because I'm too busy trying to force my ideas down his throat. I don't think this is fair, but I do want to tell him things that will help him as well as let him know that I listen to him. How can I get through to him?**

A *This is something most parents find hard. You have life experience, and want to keep your teenager safe by telling him how to avoid problems. That can mean spending more time waiting to talk than listening. Try to make sure you use your ears more than your mouth! Make a habit of listening twice as much as you speak, and don't try to jump in with 'gems of wisdom' – however well meant – about a situation before your teenager has finished talking.*

9

Fight club: how to avoid arguments, and de-escalation tactics

Arguments are a fact of life when there are teenagers in the house, and we all need coping strategies.

But could this common sign of teenage rebellion just be a sign of a healthy developing personality?

Teenagers are, by their very nature, separating from their parents. They are struggling to change from children into young adults. Teenagers are fighting (often only with themselves) to become their own people, with their own set of values, and this can bring them into conflict with their parents – and the rows begin. Although this discord is natural, it can be baffling and hurtful if you are suddenly cast in the role of 'bad guy' overnight!

Any parent of teenagers knows the scenario: you ask your son to take out the rubbish; he moans and insists a sibling should do it. You counter with repeating the request, with a mixture of irritation and frustration; he continues to

Avoid arguments about chores by offering choices instead of giving instructions. Instead of saying, 'Wash the dishes,' say 'Are you going to wash the dishes as soon as we finish dinner or after we watch the film?' This gives your teenager some control over the chore and she is less likely to feel hemmed in and complain. Note, however, you are taking it as a given that she will wash the dishes. If your teenager says she doesn't want to do either, smile and tell her that wasn't one of the choices and repeat the options.

grumble. A full scale argument erupts, with you shouting about how lazy he is and your son shouting that you spend all of your time nagging ...

Amazing. A huge argument and hurt feelings on both sides just because of a bag of rubbish. Similar rows are erupting as you read, in homes containing teenagers around the world. Knowing you are not alone might help you to accept rows as a fact of life, but what can you do to prevent them from happening in the first place?

HOW TO PRESS THE 'PAUSE' BUTTON

- Take a deep breath and think about whether this is a battle you are prepared to fight right now. You may even decide that it is a battle that is not worth fighting at all.
- Try to think about why your teenager is acting in the way he is. Does he have a good point, even if he is, possibly, expressing it in a belligerent way?

■ Did you have similar arguments with your parents? Times change, but the general nature of intergenerational warfare doesn't! Try to remember how you felt when your parents hassled you about your future/to do chores – and be honest with yourself. Take off those rose-tinted retro specs!

Is your teenage child arguing with siblings? Look at IDEA 36, *And in the blue corner ...*, for ways to deal with the problem.

Try another idea...

DAMAGE LIMITATION

You find yourself in the middle of an escalating row – so what can you do to cool the situation down?

■ Take some long, deep breaths (but make sure the exhalations don't sound like a sigh ... that could just inflame your teen further!)

■ Make sure you avoid spiralling into an all-out attack. Sometimes, when you have bottled things up for too long in the name of 'keeping the peace', you can turn any argument into a full scale attack on your teenager's life: behaviour, friends, appearance, language – it all comes flooding out! Make sure you stick to the specific topic that started the argument.

'In every dispute between parent and child, both cannot be right, but they may be, and usually are, both wrong. It is this situation which gives family life its peculiar hysterical charm.'

ISAAC ROSENFELD

Defining idea...

- Avoid overstating your case. Don't fall into the 'always' and 'never' trap – 'you never do anything without moaning'; 'you always leave the bathroom looking like a bombsite.'
- Locate the problems in the behaviour, not in your teenager. Don't tell him he is selfish for leaving a trail of his stuff round the house for you to pick up; instead, tell him he needs to clean up after himself so everyone can relax without having to do clearing up jobs all of the time.
- Encourage him to consider the impact him behaviour has on others. Explain that when he comes in late (or not at all) you stay awake worrying.
- If you feel backed into a corner, and your temper is fraying badly, you lose the ability to sort out the problem that caused the argument. You may even say things you regret. Tell your teenager that the situation is out of hand and you need to bring the discussion to a close – for now. Do not use this as a 'get out' clause – you must return to the issue soon and clear the air. A short walk or cup of coffee may, however, give you the breathing space to collect your thoughts and calm down.
- Don't be afraid to apologise if you are in the wrong – even if your point holds, apologise if you have said something hurtful.

Q **Sometimes I'm afraid to open my mouth to my teenager –
everything turns into an argument! I try to avoid rowing about
less important things, but it's getting to the point that I am not
sure when to keep my mouth shut! What can I do?**

How did it go?

A *Don't be afraid to voice your concerns about important issues – you are a
parent, and it is part of the job description to worry about your child and
the choices she makes! To avoid a row, try to make your language non-confrontational. Avoid accusations and criticism and keep your voice calm and
low. Tell your teenager that you are only concerned because you love her
– she may roll her eyes and make sarcastic comments, but the message will
eventually get through.*

Q **My teenager can say some hurtful things when we argue, and
I think she should always apologise. My wife just says I should
toughen up. Who is right?**

A *Both of you! Your teenager is hormonally wired to be rude and mean – she
is lashing out and can't really help it. Although she means it at the time,
she probably regrets it herself later. When things have cooled down, point
out that the behaviour (name calling) is unkind. Don't 'demand' an apology. It is only worth having if it is given freely.*

10

Responsibility

Do you despair about your teenager's inability to organise herself? Do you worry about the cavalier way she seems to drift from one thing to another, never seeming to worry about the future?

Why is she so irresponsible? (Clue: she's a teenager.)

Responsibility is learned over time. It is a sense of being in control of your own behaviour, and recognising that the things you do have an effect on other people. To be truly independent, a person needs to act responsibly. Children first learn to be responsible by taking care of their possessions, and perhaps caring for a pet. They gradually learn that their actions have consequences, and this begins to influence their behaviour.

As your child grows older, you offer her more responsibility to help her to develop gradually into an independent adult. As a parent, you need to guide her to behave responsibly as her independence grows. This is difficult to achieve, and ideally should happen as a continuous process from an early age. Children are best taught to be responsible via the frequent use of empowerment strategies. That means giving your child the power to make decisions, appropriate to her age. As your child grows older, you need to give her more and more power to make decisions about

Here's an idea for you… **Give your teen simple techniques to get organised – the same ones you use! Offer him a day planner or diary to make a note of appointments, club meetings, social events and birthdays. Encourage him to develop routines that will become second nature in time such as hanging up his keys by the door, laying out his clothes and school bag the night before etc.**

her life, and this can be difficult – not to say nerve wracking! To function as a young adult, your teenager needs to learn to make her own decisions, and take responsibility for them. Help her to think things through carefully by pointing out possible pitfalls and benefits offered by each of her options in any given scenario. In time, she should come to do this 'internal assessment' for herself as a matter of course when faced with making decisions.

Problems occur, however, when a child who has been shielded from the consequences of her actions by parents with the best of intentions is then expected to act in a responsible way. It is natural to want to shelter your child from the harshness of the world at large, but you may not be doing her any favours. If your child has been used to a carefree – and careless – existence you cannot expect her to change overnight into a responsible, mature person as a result of a visit from the puberty fairy. Far from it. In fact, a teenager with no sense of responsibility is like a selfish toddler on steroids – she is moody, self centred and prone to risky behaviour. That is one thing in a young child who is learning how to exit as a separate entity from her mother but another thing entirely in a teenager. Her risky behaviour will teach her lessons, in the same way as it teaches the toddler – but at what cost? Risky behaviour in teenagers can result in exposure to dangers such as alcohol abuse, drug taking and unsafe sex; a far cry from the bumped heads and grazed knees of the risk-taking toddler.

So what can you do to help your teenager to be more responsible?

- Stop doing things to get your teen out of jams she has created so she sees the consequences of her actions. When she leaves books at home she needs for school, don't run for the car keys to drop them off. If she needs clothes for the next day, let her make sure they are ready – don't do any 'emergency' washes of favourite jeans which were lying crumpled on the bedroom floor.
- This is a toughie – let consequences happen. Although it's incredibly hard to stand by and let your child mess up, and it's your natural instinct to jump in and 'make things better', restrain yourself. For example, if she's late for her after school job because she's too casual about getting there on time, she might lose it. She will learn.

Are you finding it hard to let go of the reins? Let your teen stand on his own two feet and take responsibility for himself by reading IDEA 4, *Letting go: the sharpest learning curve.*

Try another idea…

'You can learn many things from children. How much patience you have, for instance.'

FRANKLIN P. JONES

Defining idea…

43

How did it go?

Q **My husband thinks I should be less controlling of our teenage son, and allow him to make more of his own mistakes. I am worried that he will get hurt. I just want to protect him for as long as possible – life's hard enough. My husband just gets lost in some macho world where he grumbles about wanting our son to grow up to be 'a man' – whatever that means. What can I do?**

A *Behind the machismo blustering, your husband may well have a valid point. It's not about being a 'man' though; this applies to girls just as much as boys. It is important that teenagers are allowed to make mistakes; that's part of growing and changing. Unless his behaviour is potentially dangerous, try to let him go a little more and trust him to cope. He may have some difficult times as a result of the mistakes he makes, but he will learn from them, by his own experience.*

Q **I've sheltered my son from so much that I'm worried he will never be a responsible adult – and I'll not always be there to pick up the pieces! Is it too late to help him to develop a sense of responsibility?**

A *It's never too late. It may take months, or even years, for him to learn that he has to take responsibility for himself, but you can help him to achieve this. Try to back off a little and support his attempts to make decisions for himself. Scaffold his attempts at first so he has a 'safety net', but allow him to make mistakes. This is the only way he will learn that his actions have a consequence – and that is the basis for all forms of responsibility.*

11

The lump under the duvet: late nights and laziness

What's that, lurking in a pile of blankets, grunting and refusing to move?

No, it's not a monster — it's just your average teenager, refusing to get up in the morning.

If your house is like our house, you can't get your teenage son to go to bed at night – he's too busy texting friends, using the computer, or watching dodgy late films. You go to bed, telling him not to be long and hoping he won't make any noise and wake you. In the morning, the problem is reversed. Nothing short of a nuclear device is going to shift him from his warm, comfy pit.

Erratic teenage sleep patterns are often seen as resulting from peer pressure – it's just not cool to go to bed early – but annoying though this behaviour is, there may be more to it than laziness and anti social behaviour. Recent research has shown that adolescent brains do not work in the same way as adult brains – no news for parents there then! It has been suggested that older teenagers only start to produce

Here's an idea for you... **Plan your teenager's room so it is conducive to a good night's sleep. Make sure her bed is comfortable, buying a new one if necessary. Make sure her room is dark enough, with blinds and curtains if they are needed. The room should be aired regularly by leaving a window open – it not only gets rid of the smell of fusty socks; it will also bring much needed oxygen into the room.**

melatonin, a hormone that makes people feel sleepy, at around 1a.m. Adults begin to produce the hormone at around 10p.m. Researchers were unsure as to whether this was due to the general hormonal upheaval experienced by teens, or if it was caused by teenage behaviour patterns. They stay up late watching TV and playing computer games, and this stimulates brain activity (note: did the researchers actually watch any of the TV programmes involved? Most are hardly stimulating!) and exposes teenagers to bright and sometimes flashing lights, which might delay the production of melatonin.

The problem is, sleep is crucial for teenagers. They actually need more sleep than younger children and adults, but tend to get less. Newborns sleep most of the time. By the time a child is 5, he needs around eleven hours of sleep a night. By age 9 or 10, children need around nine to ten hours of sleep each night. Researchers in the late 1970s found that teenagers need ten to eleven hours sleep out of every twenty-four – yet they routinely get less, averaging six hours a night – and often less.

Lack of sleep can cause moodiness and even depression – think about it: how do you feel when you are exhausted? Teenagers who are sleep-deprived suffer from poor school performance, eating disorders, and increased drug and alcohol use.

Part of the problem may be that your teenager is not getting enough exposure to appropriately timed bright light to regulate his or her 'biological clock'. Think about his routine. During the school week, he is sleep deprived. He stays up late, but still needs to get up early for school. At the weekend, he is likely to stay up later, and you allow him to 'sleep in' on Saturdays and Sundays, because you are aware he has a sleep deficit to make up. If he emerges at around 1p.m. on Saturday, his 'biological clock' tells him the day has just started, as it is his first exposure to bright light. He misses out on valuable daylight hours, and his 'clock' is thrown out of a natural rhythm. This has a knock on effect. By Sunday night, when he tries to go to sleep at around 10p.m., he will be unable to fall asleep. Apart from being frustrating, this lack of sleep will add to his sleep deficit that carries over into the new week. The cumulative effect is a little like jet lag!

If your teenage daughter is staying in bed late, is it because she is staying out too late at night? Read IDEA 17, What time do you call this?, for more details.

Try another idea…

HOW CAN I HELP MY TEENAGER TO GET ENOUGH SLEEP?

- Try to ensure your teenager wakes at approximately the same time every day, give or take an hour or two. That includes weekends, so be prepared for a battle! This will help to regulate his 'biological clock'. Discourage 'napping'.
- Encourage your teenager to get into a night time routine. Doing the same things in the same order as you prepare for bed can set a pattern so your brain gets the message that you are preparing for sleep, so it starts to wind down.

'Without enough sleep, we all become tall two-year-olds.'
JOJO JENSEN, from *Dirt Farmer Wisdom*, 2002

Defining idea…

- Encourage regular exercise; even 20–30 minutes three times a week will help. It will help him stay healthy too. If you choose an activity you both like, such as swimming or jogging, it could be something you do together.
- Encourage relaxation before bedtime. Your teenager should avoid heavy study sessions, computer games and similar activities in the hour leading up to bed-time.
- If your teenager has a TV in his bedroom, discourage him from falling asleep with the TV on. The flickering light may inhibit a deep sleep.

How did it go?

Q   **Surely a few late nights won't make that much difference?**

A   *The odd night won't, but a disrupted sleep pattern will. Don't forget that sleep habits are hard (but not impossible) to reprogram.*

Q   **Is it a good idea to suggest a snack and a drink before bed time?**

A   *This can be part of a settling, calming routine. But eating too much, so the stomach is over-full may disrupt sleep. Make sure any snacks do not involve caffeine – and that includes chocolate and caffeinated drinks. The old standby of milk – or a malted drink – and a biscuit or two goes a long way to aid sleep! Enjoyed round 30 minutes before bedtime, this can become part of the bedtime routine, such as a warm (not hot) relaxing bath.*

12

The bank of Mum and Dad

When you have teenagers, your hand is always in your pocket for something.

But when we act like bottomless money pits, are we really doing them a disservice?

Tom Smith was seventeen when he took his father's credit card and went on a four day shopping spree – in Rome. Apparently, he was tired of the wet weather in the UK, and angry with his parents for stopping his allowance when he left his private school, deciding to take a gap year. He bought a Louis Vuitton suitcase, a Prada coat, Versace trousers and Dolce & Gabbana jeans. His shopping spree racked up an amazing £12,000 on his father's plastic.

Now, that was a true story, and hopefully it puts your own teenager's spending in perspective. But it is a fact of life; teenagers are expensive to run. If you add together clothing allowances, driving lessons, computers, pocket money and entertainment, you could run a sports car for the same cost as your teenager – and it wouldn't answer back!

Here's an idea for you... **If your teenager asks for something special – an electric guitar, hi-fi equipment, an iPod – sit him down and talk about strategies for getting the object of his desire. You may be willing to give him part of the purchase price, perhaps as a birthday present. Then help him to work out how to come up with the rest of the money – saving pocket money, doing extra chores, getting a part time job – and help him to shop around to get the best deal. And if he has managed to buy the object of his desires, he's likely to treasure it more because of the effort involved in obtaining it.**

Clothes and other style accessories, already increasingly important with pre teens, are even more important with teenagers. Clothes of a certain type – usually expensive, and with particular designer labels – can seem to help them fit in with their peers at school. But it does not have to be that way. I can honestly say that neither of my teenagers has ever whined for designer labels. It's a good job really, because they wouldn't have got them. That sounds harsh, but stop and think for a minute. What life lesson are we teaching our children if we tacitly buy into the idea that to fit in, we all need to be the same? What does it teach them if we subscribe to the idea that designer clothing with overblown price tags makes the people who wear them better somehow than the people who don't? Encourage your teens to value individuality and they will reject the more crass parts of our consumer culture. My son is keen on vintage clothing and haunts charity shops and thrift stores to find unique jackets and shoes. My daughter loves to customise clothing to fit her own desires. It's a win-win situation: they feel unique; I don't waste money on designer labels.

POCKET MONEY AND ALLOWANCES

An allowance given on a weekly – or better, a monthly – basis will help your teenager to appreciate the value of money, and teach her to manage a budget. It will help her to decide if she wants to blow it all straight away – and face a lean month; save some for a special purchase, or manage the money evenly so it lasts. We give our teenagers their money monthly in a lump sum. It is expected to cover a monthly bus pass and lunches as well as recreational spending. Our daughter ekes her money out carefully with the odd spree. Our son spends it rather more quickly and faces a lean time as the month draws to a close. A 'top up' would no doubt be welcome, but it would teach him that blowing his money is OK because someone will always pick up the pieces. They are learning about how to spend money responsibly, and the consequences of not doing so, before it really matters. Not having enough money left to go to the pictures is one thing; not having enough money to pay your bills is another thing entirely.

If you give your child an allowance in this way, be very clear about what it is expected to cover. We do not expect our teenagers to buy all of their clothes from their allowance and still foot the bill for general clothes. Special 'fashion' items – clubwear etc. – is to come from their own pockets, however.

Is your teen expecting you to bale him out when he makes expensive mistakes? Look at IDEA 10, *Responsibility*, to find ways to make him take more responsibility.

Try another idea...

'It is not giving children more that spoils them; it is giving them more to avoid confrontation.'
    JOHN GRAY, author of *Children Are From Heaven*

Defining idea...

How did it go?

Q **My teenager says all his friends get more pocket money than he does, but I can't afford to give him any more. What should I do?**

A *Firstly, tell him straight out that you cannot afford to give him more; your budget is used up. I would advocate showing him bills so he can see how much it costs to run a house – he will be amazed. Secondly, teenagers always say their friends have it easier than they do – they do fewer chores, can stay out later, wear more make up etc. – tell him you will discuss the matter with some of your friends to find out what they give their children; it is likely to be no more than you give. Remember, anyway, this is not a competition. You give what you can and what you think is enough. It sounds like a T shirt slogan, but he should perhaps be reminded that pocket money is not a right; it's a privilege!*

Q **My teenager wants expensive designer trainers. I think the cheaper ones are just as good quality and resent paying for a 'name.' Am I being mean?**

A *Not at all. Throw the ball back into his court: tell him you will give him the cost of the cheaper trainers, and if he wants the more expensive ones he can save up his pocket money or work to pay the difference. If he is not willing to do this, he has the price of the cheaper pair.*

13

Cyber safety: the potential dangers for your computer-obsessed teen

Computers have revolutionised the teen world. They are a vital source of chat, messages and gaming – and even help them with their homework!

When does a teenager's use of computers and the Internet stop being fun, and start being a cause for concern?

There's no doubt about it; personal computers have changed the way we live. This is even more so for your teen. He spends hours surfing, chatting and shopping, and even sometimes finds time to use educational sites …

Unfortunately, as with every source of information, there is a lot of unsuitable material out there on the Internet. You must guard your young teen in the same way as a younger child from exposure to some of the more unsavoury aspects of cyberspace.

Here's an idea for you… **Encourage your daughter to choose a neutral name for use in chatrooms etc. that does not let people know her gender. This can avoid a great deal of random harassment, and help her to remain anonymous. It offers some protection and allows her to retain some control over her experiences on the Internet.**

You will know yourself about the dangers as your own inbox fills with exhortations to view all manner of pornography from the imaginative to the totally bizarre. These spam emails can appear on any computer; email addresses are harvested and bought from other sites – mostly nothing to do with pornography. Invest in a spam filter (sounds gross – but it's nothing to do with meat products, and it's very useful!) to help to sieve out the unwanted addresses. You can also buy software 'guardians' which will prevent your teen from coming across or accessing unsuitable 'adult orientated' sites. Even the most innocuous of searches on the Internet can make hideous and unsuitable sites pop up – I recently did a search for an educational book I was writing about reptiles, and you can only imagine the lists of bizarre porn sites that appeared as I typed in my research questions about crocodiles …

Spam filters screen out unsuitable material, often by using keywords. This type of programme can protect your email account from the worst sites, and applying parental controls can give you *some* sense of security. However, with children and young teens, keep Internet enabled computers in a public room so you can monitor their activity. Sometimes teens can find themselves surfing innocently into murkier parts of the Internet, and if you are around to notice you can pre-empt problems.

Worried about your children's safety? Look at IDEA 48, *Safe as houses – teaching your teen about personal safety*, for ways to keep them safe.

Try another idea...

DEVELOPING INTERNET SAVVY

Talk to your child about the potential dangers of the World Wide Web. In today's technological world, it's right up there with the 'stranger danger' talk. Make them aware that:

- Some websites ask for personal information, such as names, postal address, e-mail address, and even profile information such as age, gender etc. Your child should *never* fill in this information without checking with you.
- Always ask before downloading anything – games, wallpaper etc. They may be downloading spyware along with fun, which can track sites visited. Viruses can

'Adolescence is a period of rapid changes. Between the ages of 12 and 17, for example, a parent ages as much as 20 years.'
AL BERNSTEIN

Defining idea...

55

also infect your computer as they are brought in attached to downloaded material. Always run an anti virus programme, firewall and a programme designed to seek out and destroy spyware.

■ If your teen has a website or is a member of a web community, make sure he does not include his home address, telephone number or other personal information.

■ Anyone – including people who would exploit teenagers – can set up their own website. Be cautious – people may not be who they say they are.

■ Be especially cautious about chatrooms. They can be fun – but they can also be dangerous. We have all heard horror stories of teens being lured into meeting older, sexually exploitative people who they have met in chatrooms. It pays to be careful. Your teen should never say anything he would not say in a public place, where he could be overheard. Chatrooms are sometimes used by sexual predators to groom victims. They may profess to be someone completely different, such as another teenager. Your teen must understand that he should NEVER agree to meet up somewhere with someone he has 'met' online.

■ Instant messaging (IM) is a great, convenient way of getting in touch with people – but your teen needs to be careful. Some IM services require a 'profile' with personal information. Profiles can help your teen to make new friends – but it can also leave him open to harassment. Make sure that your teen knows that he can block people and not receive messages from them if they are abusive.

Q **My teenage daughter never looks up from the computer. She even neglects her schoolwork. What can I do?**

How did it go?

A *This is a common complaint! It is perhaps this generation's equivalent to the hours we spent on the phone to our school friends. Talk to her about it. You may need to set some limits for time spent on the computer. Where school is concerned, check school guidelines about how long it should take, and make sure she spends this amount of time on her work. You may need to introduce a 'probationary period' where your daughter shows you her completed homework before she is allowed computer access.*

Q **Where can I find out more about Internet safety?**

A *As well as at home where you can monitor her activity, your teenage daughter will be using the Internet at school, at friends' houses, in the library or even Internet cafes. You cannot always be there, to ensure she takes safety messages on board. You can find out more about how to keep your daughter safe by downloading a great safety booklet from: http://www.missingkids.com/adcouncil/pdf/talk/teensafety_eng.pdf*

14

Making time

Are you resources rich but time poor? Are you spoiling your kid to make up for your absence?

However busy your life is, your kids should be your number one priority. More than any career, happy well-adjusted children are your most important 'achievement'.

There are so many demands on your time – work, commuting, shopping, house-work – that it can be hard to make time to be a family, just hanging about, not necessarily doing much. Some of the best, most valuable 'family time' is not had when we are on planned trips or outings, but just rattling around the house, per-haps doing jobs together, eating together or watching a film. Incidental chat – the unplanned, no pressure conversation that goes on in these circumstances – is what cements families together. You cannot expect to suddenly launch into major discus-sions about sex, the future, curfew etc. if your teenager is not used to you talking to her on a day to day basis.

Many parents simply do not make time to listen to their teenage children. Think about it – when was the last time you really listened to yours? Be honest; can you

Here's an idea for you…

You'll find that if you don't actually ring fence time to spend as a family, it won't happen. It doesn't have to be an 'official' time, as that can get forced. But make sure that every single week, you do something together. Why not cook a meal with your teenagers? Apart from giving you time to talk, it can be great fun. Make it something that entails lots of chopping, slicing and other time consuming preparations and it will really create a sense of something achieved together. It may even teach him how to make a few meals!

name her favourite group or groups? What are her friends called? What subjects is she studying at school – and is she having any difficulties? What films has she seen or books has she read lately, and what did she think of them? If you talked on a day to day basis, you would know the answers to at least some of these questions.

The relationship you have with your teenagers is the same as any other relationship; it requires work and thoughtfulness to maintain it properly. In the same way as you cannot fob off your spouse or partner with even the biggest box of chocolates to make up for habitually neglecting them, you cannot 'buy off' your teenager with expensive gifts. That is not to say she will not accept the designer train-

ers/iPod/MP3 player you throw at her; she is only human. But she knows she is being short changed when gifts are given instead of time. You may be buying gifts to show your love for her, but it doesn't work. She is more likely to see it as a guilt offering to make up for all the time you spend working instead of enjoying her company.

Are you making time to communicate with your teenager? Read IDEA 8, *Learning to listen: how to open channels of communication***, for ideas on how to communicate.**

Try another idea…

It sounds corny, but the greatest gift you can give your teenager – or children of any age – is your time. There is no point in complaining that she does not want to spend time with you because she is busy with her friends at the very time you choose to bestow some attention on her – why should she change her plans to accommodate you? Of course, if she is getting all of her companionship and emotional support from her peers, you may not be keen on the messages and values she absorbs from them – but you cannot complain if you have not been around to support her. Make sure that you schedule in family time amongst your other commitments – it's hard, but it pays dividends. That does not mean time spent doing chores – a necessary evil! – but rather time spent chatting, going on outings, watching TV together etc. These seemingly 'incidental' times are often the times your daughter feels relaxed enough to tell you about her day. Don't force the issue, and make her spend time in your company if it is not something you normally do; let it develop organically, after a little nudge from you.

'Your children need your presence more than your presents.'

JESSE JACKSON

Defining idea…

Q **I feel pulled in so many directions – work, home, young children, spouse and teenage son – that I don't know how to fit everybody's needs in, let alone my own! I just don't see how I can set aside special time for my teenager every week.**

A *If you don't, you may well regret it for years to come. Your teenage son will soon leave home; your small children will grow up. You cannot reclaim time that is lost. The relationship you build with your son now will develop into the adult to adult relationship you will enjoy after he leaves home. You don't need to make Herculean efforts – just be around for him. Think about the possibility of cutting back a few hours at work if possible to spend longer with your family. Or just rent a DVD, make some snacks and settle down together – it gives you a rest, too!*

Q **Would it be too corny to try to take up a hobby that I can enjoy along with my teenage son, to bring us closer?**

A *Not at all! Without labouring the point, find something you can do together. It could be a spectator sport (my teens and their dad are all season ticket holders at Newcastle United – that gives them something to share on a regular basis). My son also enjoys strategy games such as Warhammer, and that's something we can play together. It could just as easily be computer games, fishing, running – just find something that you can both genuinely enjoy and look forward to as special shared time.*

15

Driving passions

Getting a driver's license is a rite of passage, and a cause for celebration.

But with two out of five deaths among US teens being the result of a motor vehicle crash, it's also a source of great anxiety for parents.

Getting a driver's license is, for many teenagers, a key to the adult world of independence. Once they have their license, you no longer have to do the driving. They can go where they want, when they want – subject to you handing over the keys!

Driving is an incredibly useful skill. I, like many others, sometimes view my car as an extension of my body and feel lost without it. However, this blessing can seem more like a curse if your teenage son is the one behind the wheel. The first time he drives off, all the shock-horror drink driving campaign advertisements play luridly in your head as you smile a rictus smile. But are your fears well founded?

Teens are *statistically* more likely to crash than older drivers. They are most likely to crash during the first year after passing their tests. This is possibly due to inexperi-

Here's an idea for you... **Schedule a defensive driving course for your teenager after she has passed her test. Even though she drives correctly, she needs to be able to anticipate the actions and mistakes that other drivers make out on the road.**

ence. They are less likely to be able to identify and cope with hazardous situations than more experienced drivers.

Your teenager will start his driving career with little technical ability. Even after passing a driving test, actually learning to drive competently takes time. It is practice that makes a driver capable of good judgement and decision making.

Teenagers are statistically more likely than older and more experienced drivers to speed, drive after drinking alcohol or ride in a car driven by someone who has been drinking alcohol. They are more likely to drive through a red light, and less likely to wear a seat belt. They are also more likely than older drivers to behave in a risk taking manner – perhaps due to their brains' immaturity. As teenagers, they are more likely generally to be impulsive and take risks – and in a car, this type of behaviour can be fatal.

Teenagers are likely to do a lot of driving at night, to social events and the houses of friends. They are also likely to have a car full of friends. Both of these factors increase the likelihood of problems as the car may be noisy and the driver may be distracted. A larger percentage of fatal crashes involving teenage drivers are single-vehicle crashes, where the vehicle has left the road and hit a tree or pole, or the car has overturned.

WHAT CAN I DO TO HELP KEEP MY TEEN SAFE?

The key to safe driving is lots of practice and experience. Help your teenager by accompanying him on a regular basis so that he has a chance to develop the habits and skills he needs to be a safe driver.

- Accompany him to give him experience with driving in adverse weather conditions, and at night.
- Insist on general safety rules such as the wearing of seat belts; a no alcohol rule (not even a legal 'safe' amount).
- Come to an agreement about when he is allowed to carry passengers. It may be worth waiting until he has a little experience.
- Impress upon him the dangers of driving when tired.
- Be a good example. Be a courteous driver yourself, and do not indulge in 'road-rage'-promoting gestures or shout obscenities when driving! Your children will pick up all your driving habits – including the bad ones!
- Talk to your teenager about the dangers that distractions such as loud music and eating food whilst driving present and of course talk about the reasons why mobile phones are banned from use whilst driving.

If your teen is learning to drive, it may be time to lay down some rules. Read IDEA 24, *Rules of the house*, for some guidelines.

Try another idea...

'The one thing that unites all human beings, regardless of age, gender, religion, economic status or ethnic background, is that, deep down inside, we ALL believe that we are above average drivers.'
DAVE BARRY, author of *Things That It Took Me 50 Years to Learn*

Defining idea...

- If your teen is taking medication or has any medical illness, check with your family doctor about any effects they may have on his ability to drive.

How did it go?

Q My daughter has passed her test – surely that proves she is a safe driver. Why should I still go out with her when she drives?

A You need to be sure she has sufficient experience and that her driving skills are up to scratch. The old adage 'You've passed your test – now learn how to drive!' is guaranteed to annoy her, but there is truth in the old saying. It is experience that makes a good driver, not a piece of paper that says she drove well enough 'on the day.'

Q My teenage children regularly borrow my car. Are there any additional safety checks I should carry out on the vehicle to maximise their safety?

A You need to make sure that your vehicle is in a safe condition for any driver – including you! On a regular basis, reassure yourself that the brakes are responding well and not binding, and check your tyre pressures and tread. You could add an essential emergency pack in case of difficulties – a flashlight, warning triangle, the telephone number for your automobile assistance organisation, jump leads, foot pump etc. and explain to your teenagers what the pack contains and how to use the items. I also include a shovel in the winter, as well as a Hessian sack for those days when a de-icer is just not enough – and it has saved me from getting stuck on several occasions!

16

Punk princess or just plain peculiar? Avoiding confrontation about style

The true test of whether you are in touch with your 'inner teenager' comes when your teenage daughter appears wearing extreme fashions, with magenta hair or psychedelically coloured make up.

How do you react?

Trawl your memory. Can you remember your own mother and father being horrified by your make up and hair 'experiments'? I can. I was a great fan of big hair (it was the 1980s) and my make up had to be seen to be believed. At 15, my *maquillage* was less 'Breakfast Club' than 'Dog's Breakfast'. I wore a huge range of sparkly colours, artfully (I thought) applied all at once, along with thick eyeliner and mascara. Hideous. I have the photos to prove it. My parents coped; now it is my turn.

Try to remember that your daughter is going through a 'discovery' phase. She's trying to work out who she is, and may try on new personas on a weekly basis!

Think about why you wear make up, if you do. I wear it to make myself feel more attractive and confident. I have a different 'face' for a party than I do for a business meeting – and your teenager is trying to find her 'faces' by trying different styles.

Remember to take a deep breath whenever you feel the need to comment on your daughter's make up or hair. Does it really matter what she looks like? With a young teen, you need to make sure she is not looking too 'adult' and obviously over sexualised. There is plenty of time for sparkly belly exposing tops and skin tight jeans later.

Here's an idea for you...

If you find your daughter's make up application a little heavy handed for daytime use, try to show her the difference between a casual gloss and full 'going out' war paint. What is great fun is taking turns – you make up your daughter and let her do your make up. If you are feeling brave, agree to go out for a coffee in your full regalia! To take the 'wimp-out' option, you could just book a mother–daughter makeover with a make up artist at a store cosmetic counter. Not so much fun, and fewer giggles, but it's still a bonding experience.

With an older teen, you can comment all you want – but she might not listen. Remember, your daughter has friends and they have houses too, where she can get ready to go out without you ever seeing what she looks like …

HAIR WE GO …

Imagine three teens: one, during the punk era, had his red hair held aloft with severe back combing and industrial strength gel; a second sported long, foppishly curly hair that was like something from *Flock of Seagulls* crossed with a refugee from *Brideshead Revisited*. The third transformed her previously glossy raven locks with an interesting 'long at the back; shaved in at the sides' combo. Despite their strange *dos*, these were great teens with social consciences who all grew up to be the respectable professionals they are today (my husband and his siblings). Their sanguine mother reassured herself that whatever odd changes took place in their appearance, they were the same good people – and you must do the same if and when your teenager wears clothes, make up or hairstyles that you don't like. You aren't supposed to!

If you've said some harsh things about your teen's appearance, check out IDEA 39, *Take it back! Saying things you regret*, for solutions.

Try another idea…

Don't let yourself worry about 'what people will think'; if they are shallow enough to judge your teenage children by their appearance, rather than by the way they act, do you really care about their opinions? Whatever the generation, since teenagers have been in existence, they have tried to shock their elders with extreme styles from Teddy Boy D.A.s and lacquered beehives through Biba false eyelashes and hippy haircuts; punk Mohicans and bondage wear to 'long time dead' Goth styling. It pays to contextualise. Teens use their styles to feel part of the crowd – or conversely, to feel 'different'. It's a stage they go through, and a healthy one at that.

Basically, just keep reminding yourself that however extreme you find your teenager's style, it will pass. Whatever the package, it's the same kid inside. She may look scary; he may look hairy, but it's what's on the inside that matters.

'The needs of children during adolescence are particular and acute. They need an opportunity to develop a sense of identity and to maintain the sense of security that emanates from group acceptance.'

ELLIOT W. EISNER

Defining idea…

How did it go?

Q **My teenage son is into heavy metal and wears his hair long and scruffy. He wears awful T shirts with offensive pictures and I hate it. We row about it all of the time. What can I do?**

A *Pause for a moment – why are you getting so upset? Your son's style is a statement of identity and a sign of belonging in his peer group. It's important to him, and he will eventually grow out of it. Why let unimportant things spoil your relationship? You would be well advised to swallow your objections and save your 'big guns' for important matters, such as health and relationships.*

Q **My youngest son is 14 and refuses to wash his hair. He thinks it looks fluffy when he washes it. I can't bear seeing him with greasy hair – it looks like he doesn't care about his appearance. What can I do?**

A *Buy him some special, gorgeous smelling 'manly' products of his own – conditioner as well as shampoo. Reassure him that the conditioner will help his hair to lay flat and will avoid the bouffant look he hates. Remind him that girls like men who look after themselves ... and that includes washing their hair! Make it clear that he must wash his hair at least once a week, and that is not negotiable, on grounds of hygiene.*

17

What time do you call this?

Lying awake in the early hours listening for the key in the door interferes with the sleep patterns of parents around the world.

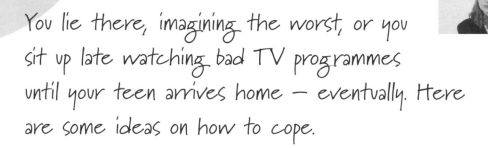

You lie there, imagining the worst, or you sit up late watching bad TV programmes until your teen arrives home — eventually. Here are some ideas on how to cope.

When your children are smaller, you know where they are. Once they become teenagers, their social lives focus increasingly on evening activities, and decisions about curfews and staying in touch need to be taken.

A curfew gives your teen a chance to experience a degree of independence within a support structure. You reach a compromise whereby you are recognising that your teen is getting older and more mature, but you still retain some peace of mind.

WHERE IS MY TEEN?

This is, perhaps, a more important issue than what time your child has to come home. You need to know where your son will be when he is out with his friends.

When you go out, tell your teenager where you are going and give her a contact number (or take your mobile phone). Give her an idea of the time you will be back, and if your plans change give her a call. If you model thoughtful behaviour to her – letting the people who love you know where you are and what time you will be back – she is more likely to see its value and treat you in the same way.

Ask him to leave you a phone number too, if he is at a friend's house 'in case of emergencies'. This is helpful for the many occasions when his mobile phone is turned off, or has run out of charge ... I have been very glad that I have made a list of my children's friend's home phone numbers on many occasions when I have been trying to track them down!

With young teens, it is especially important to know about where they are. If they are at the cinema, or a friend's house that is one thing; hanging around at the shops or in the park is another. 'Hanging out' time, doing nothing with friends, is a necessary and enjoyable part of being a teenager. However, if that is all your teen is doing, boredom can set it – and peer pressure can take over, spilling over into risky behaviour such as drinking. Set boundaries that make you comfortable, and discuss your reasons with your teenager. He may not like your decisions, but at least he will know where you are coming from – rather than thinking you are being randomly mean, just for the fun of it!

A good rule to apply with young teens is this: if you change locations, text home. If he moves from the shopping centre to go to the cinema, for example. He may be embarrassed about calling – whether you think he should or not is neither here nor there. You do not want to make your son feel like a social pariah (or, god forbid, a nerd ...). Texting is more acceptable, as he is likely to have his thumbs permanently welded to his phone anyway; he doesn't have to 'fess up that he is texting his mum...

If your teen's out partying all night, look at IDEA 35, *24-hour party people*, for ways to cope.

Try another idea...

CREATING CURFEWS

It is worth discussing curfew with your teenager rather than telling him an arbitrary time; it is also likely to create the least resistance. The actual time you decide upon depends upon your child and your family situation. For a younger teenager, the time will obviously be earlier than for an older one. You may decide on a school night curfew with a later time at weekends. If your son is responsible and sensible, he is likely to be able to cope with a later curfew than if he is less responsible and prone to recklessness. Of course, teenagers mature at different rates, and you know your own children so you are the person best positioned to decide on the curfew that suits both them and you. Involve your teen in making the final decision and listen to his ideas before you come to a decision.

WHAT DO I DO IF HE DOESN'T KEEP HIS CURFEW?

Enforcing a curfew takes persistence – and sometimes lack of sleep! If your son is late once, find out why. If he has called to let you know why, and has a valid excuse, cut him some slack. If he is deliberately ignoring curfew, it is a different matter. Explain again that it makes you worry, and insist that if he does not come in on time there will be sanctions. An earlier curfew the next time he goes out – cut by the amount of time he was late – is, perhaps, one solution; repeated lateness may need stronger sanctions such as grounding.

'I have noticed that the people who are late are often so much jollier than the people who have to wait for them.'

E. V. LUCAS, author

Defining idea...

How did it go?

Q **My 14-year-old has a curfew of 9pm unless I am picking her up from somewhere. She constantly complains that other kids are allowed out much later. What should I do?**

A *The 'my friends are allowed to ...' card is the oldest trick in the book! Don't be guilt tripped into a later curfew – it is your decision, to suit your family. You have to be comfortable with the situation. You cannot blame your daughter for trying, and promise you will revisit the curfew time decision as she gets older.*

Q **Why should I discuss the setting of a curfew with my daughter? It's my decision as parent.**

A *Firstly, you will be showing you respect her and her ability to make decisions. Being dictatorial will not allow her to develop decision making skills and it disempowers her. When you discuss things with your teenager she will accept it as being more fair, because she has ownership of the process. That will make it more likely that she will keep to the rules! That does not mean you should be afraid to make rules, however. Remember that the final decision rests with you – but if you are dictatorial about the way you set curfew, your daughter is more likely to rebel and you will store up trouble for yourself. Gently, easy is better!*

18

Just say no – *please*? Your teenager and drugs

If you think your child is using drugs, your natural reaction may be to panic.

But despite the media stories about teenagers taking drugs, getting addicted and overdosing, try to remember that for most youngsters, taking illegal drugs is not part of normal everyday life. Just because you find a roach, it doesn't mean your daughter is a drug addict!

Nobody wants their teenager to take drugs. We tend to think about drugs education as telling our kids horror stories – and there are many – so they won't take them. This is a valid viewpoint, but perhaps it is not the most helpful for your teen.

Here's an idea for you... **The better informed you are about drugs and their effects the more credibility your teenager will give your views. Find out about the effects of drugs on the Internet, or by picking up a booklet at your local health centre. A useful and informative website may be found at: http://www.drugs-info.co.uk/drugpages/drugsindex.htm**

Although it is tempting to hide behind the idea that 'all drugs are evil', your teen needs to know the facts so she can make a responsible decision, and there are some things you must try to share with her in a calm manner – hopefully when she is a young teenager. If you leave it too long, you may be too late.

- Nobody can be sure exactly what they are taking – drug dealers often cut drugs with different substances that can be almost as dangerous as the drugs themselves.
- Drug takers are never sure of the strength of the drug they are taking; this can lead to accidental overdose.
- You cannot be sure of the effect a drug will have on any given day – even if you have taken it before.

- It is dangerous to mix alcohol and drugs, and different types of drug.
- Needles and syringes can spread killer diseases such as HIV and hepatitis B or C.
- If a child is caught in possession of a controlled drug she has committed a criminal offence, and this will be recorded by the police. This may bar her from certain jobs, and visiting other countries.

If your teen is overusing alcohol as well as dabbling in drugs, take a look at IDEA 19, *The demon drink: your teen and alcohol*, for solutions.

Try another idea…

HOW DO I KNOW?

You may read articles or leaflets that tell you to look for 'tell-tale signs' that your teenager is taking drugs. Unfortunately, there is no such thing. The 'tell-tale signs' could easily be applied to most teens at one time or another! The main thing to look out for is sudden change. The behaviour described below may – but may not – make it more likely that your teen is taking drugs. The only sure way to find out is to talk to her, in a non-confrontational way, to find out what is going on.

- Sudden and dramatic mood swings.
- Hostility towards family members.
- Out of character behaviour.
- Suddenly dropping old friends for a new group.
- Loss of interest in personal care and appearance.
- Suddenly altered sleeping and eating patterns.
- Unusual smells on clothing.

'Drugs are a waste of time. They destroy your memory and your self respect and everything that goes along with your self esteem.'
KURT COBAIN, singer

Defining idea…

77

IF MY TEEN IS TAKING DRUGS, WHAT CAN I DO?

Teenagers take drugs for many reasons. Poor self esteem; peer pressure – wanting to fit in and seem 'grown up'; a desire to rebel; boredom; curiosity; or because they feel stressed and pressured.

If you suspect your teenager is taking drugs, try to hold back from making snap judgments. Resist the urge to snoop in her bedroom – even if you found something, how could you bring the subject up when you had been doing something under-hand? Try to talk through what has happened – what has she been taking, and does she know why? Wait until you can be calm (at least outwardly) and say, 'I think we need to talk. I'm worried that you might be using drugs. Will you tell me what's happening?' You may be able to offer alternative ways of dealing with any problems that may have triggered the drug taking. Let your child know you love and support her, but let her know you disapprove of the drug-taking behaviour. Does she know the risks?

You can also contact your doctor or one of the drug helplines listed at the back of the book for advice. Do not feel ashamed or that you are exposed as a bad parent; the fact that your teen has chosen to take drugs is not your personal responsibility. Children from all different backgrounds experiment with drugs.

Q   **I smoked dope in college but don't any longer. Surely it's no big deal if my teen experiments?**

How did it go?

A   *This is a personal choice, and many people have the same experience as you. Be aware that there are some long-term effects associated with regular marijuana use:*

- *If smoked, the smoke contains even more carcinogens and tar than regular cigarette smoke, so there are increased risks of cancer, emphysema and ulcers.*
- *It can depress your immune system.*
- *It has been linked to psychosis such as schizophrenia.*
- *It can cause poor concentration and memory loss.*

Q   **I found what I think is some speed (amphetamines) when I was washing my 18-year-old son's jeans. He's a really sensible boy usually – what can I do? I'm in a bit of a panic.**

A   *Try to be calm, and ask your son in a non accusing way (if you can manage it – this is a tall order!) what the substance is. If he tells you it is speed, ask him why he feels the need to use it. Are there other ways he can address his problems, if he has any? Make sure he knows that speed is notoriously impure, and is often cut with a variety of substances from scouring powder to brick dust. Be sure he knows the risks of taking amphetamines, such as heart problems, insomnia, psychosis and dependency. You cannot make him give up the drug, but you can try to influence him. Suggest a visit to a drugs counsellor to help address the problem.*

The demon drink: your teen and alcohol

For most teens, alcohol is the number one drug of choice. They use it without thinking twice, and see it all around them on sale in supermarkets, corner shops and restaurants. They see it used by their parents at home.

So how do we teach them that alcohol is in fact a potentially dangerous drug, to be treated with caution?

Teenagers use alcohol more frequently and in greater quantities than all other drugs combined. The danger is that we turn a blind eye to most drinking behaviour in our teenage children, relieved that it is 'only' alcohol, rather than illegal drugs such as cannabis or cocaine. Just because society condones drinking (but not in teenagers) it does not mean that alcohol should be treated lightly, however; it is a powerful mood altering drug.

Apart from direct health risks from alcohol consumption, risk taking behaviour, (always prevalent in teens), is magnified by alcohol consumption. Teenagers are

Here's an idea for you... **It is virtually inevitable that your teen will drink alcohol at some point, so teach her to drink responsibly. Teach her to 'pace' herself, alternating alcoholic drinks with mineral water or juice. Advise her to have a starchy meal such as pasta before going to a party and tell her never to drink on an empty stomach. Encourage her to plan what she would do if she found herself in a dangerous situation due to drink – to look out for friends who may be drunk and to ring home if she gets into difficulties.**

more likely, for example, to indulge in unsafe sexual behaviour after drinking, increasing their risk of exposure to STDs, pregnancy, casual sex and even rape.

In the US alone, approximately 1,700 college students die from alcohol-related injuries every year. Young people who have consumed alcohol are twice as likely to fall from a height and need medical care, and are a terrifying 75% more likely to be sexually victimised. They are more likely to become involved in fights, and to be involved in road accidents. In 1999, a quarter of drivers or passengers killed or injured in road accidents had blood alcohol concentration over the legal limit for driving.

If your teenager comes home drunk, try to stay calm. Creating a scene won't help; he is not even in a fit state to cope with a rational discussion. Make sure he drinks some water and get him to bed. Give him a basin in case he vomits in the night. If he does, make sure he cleans up after himself – he needs to see the consequences of his actions. The next day, talk to your teenager about the situation. Explain why getting drunk is risky behaviour, and remind him that he feels ill precisely because he drank too much. It may be that he did not intend to drink so much that he became drunk, and his inexperience allowed it to happen. The experience should be looked upon as something to learn from.

Alcohol can lead to risk taking behaviour. Read IDEA 5, *Why are they so weird?*, to find out why teenagers behave in this way.

Try another idea…

BINGE DRINKING

There is presently a moral panic about 'binge drinking' among young people – and some would say, with just cause. 'Binge drinking' is identified as drinking more than six units of alcohol at one time for women, and eight for men. Alcohol is available very cheaply and is easy to purchase; many pubs and clubs offer highly discounted drinks, specially targeting the young drinker. Whether you like it or not, older teens come into this category, and many teenagers organise their social life around alcohol.

If you feel your teen is binge drinking, gently talk to him about the health risks he is taking. Ensure that he knows that alcohol is a neurotoxin – that means it can actually poison your brain. Binge drinking depletes Vitamin B, which is necessary for brain function. Regular binge drinking can even lead to alcohol related brain damage. This can cause permanent memory loss, tremors and difficulties with balance. That is apart from the damage that can be done to the liver, and the increase in risk of mouth and throat cancers.

'Drunkenness is nothing but voluntary madness.'
SENECA

Defining idea…

Q   **My 16-year-old daughter goes out in a crowd that visits pubs and clubs. She is under age, but my wife thinks I'm being too strict when I tell her she is not allowed to go. Do you think there is a compromise?**

A   *This is a really tough decision. In all likelihood, if you ban her she will be tempted to go behind your back – and she will be legally allowed to drink in pubs and clubs soon. Instead, explain why you are concerned – and don't forget to tell her that under-age drinking is illegal. Emphasise the need for personal safety, and remind her that alcohol can lead even the most sensible people to do silly things such as take unreasonable risks physically and sexually. Try to keep a dialogue going so you stay aware of her social habits.*

Q   **My 19-year-old son is a regular binge drinker, and he has told me that he is starting to feel as though he has a drinking problem. How can I help him?**

A   *You should feel proud of your son, that he is mature enough to recognise that he has a problem – and that he feels safe enough with you to tell you about it. Wherever you are in the world, there are groups and healthcare professionals who can offer support. Consult your family doctor, who can act as a portal for other services. Alternatively, many self-help support groups allow people to self refer. Your son will need a great deal of support – and you may too, as living with alcohol addiction is emotionally exhausting.*

20

Let's talk about sex, baby

Young people who are able to talk with their parents about sex tend to delay having sex and are more likely to use contraception when they do.

So, despite the fact that you may not want to think about your teen as a sexual being — and she finds the idea of you having sex repugnant — what are you waiting for? Get talking!

Ideally, you should begin talking to your child about sex – in terms of 'where babies come from' – when she is quite young. Introducing the subject well before your child reaches puberty means many of the 'mechanics' are out of the way before the difficult part – the emotions that sex can create – kicks in with puberty. Remember, sexual education is not just keeping your child safe, although this is a very important factor. It is also about offering her the opportunity to grow up comfortable with her own sexuality so she is able to develop close, loving and rewarding relationships with her partners as she grows into adulthood.

Here's an idea for you…

If you aren't sure how to broach the subject of sexual relationships with your teen, use everyday media to start conversations. TV programmes, soaps and magazines, often aimed at teens, frequently contain sexual issues, sometimes at quite an explicit level. This can give you a hook to hang your discussion on – how does your teen think the character felt? Could they have handled the situation in a different way? You can explore ideas in this way, 'once removed', and that may make you both feel more comfortable.

I have talked about sex with my children as a part of everyday life, answering their questions and offering information at a level that suits their development. This is much better – and less embarrassing for the child – than a sit down, one-off talk. My eldest daughter was telling me the other day about a discussion she had with friends at school where they were talking about 'the talk' their parents gave them about sex – and she could not pinpoint any particular occasion. Drip feeding, talking about sex and sexual feelings as and when appropriate, seems far more natural to me; the child learns at her level and does not have information forced upon her before she is ready or interested. This is child centred sex education, and keeping the discussion going in this way as your child enters her teens ensures you stay in touch with her life and emotions. This sort of almost incidental sex education means that discussion of sex and relationships is integrated into everyday life rather than being made something to get hung up about – just as sex and relationships are integrated into our everyday lives as adults.

Try to keep an open mind as you talk to your teen about sex – even if you are shocked by her attitudes or values, which may not be yours. For example, if your son talks in a way that shows a lack of respect for girls and women (and this is particularly true of younger male teens who are perhaps trying too hard to be 'manly') or stereotypical attitudes, remind him that he has female friends, relatives etc. – do they fit these rather one dimensional views? Would he want other boys to think of his sister in this way? This makes women more 'human', and will encourage him to see them as people rather than just bodies.

By the time your child is a teenager, you should be introducing the idea that sexual relationships should involve a sense of responsibility; that sexual relationships involve caring and emotional responsibility towards another person. Teens need to understand that a sexual relationship should only be considered when both partners feel comfortable enough with one another to talk about their feelings, what contraception they will use and if they have any doubts. If they don't feel they can cope with this, they are not really mature enough to be having sex. Empowering your teen by sharing information and having open discussions about sexual matters makes it less likely that she will be pressured into having sex by the views of her peers or a potential partner.

If you feel as though you are not coping with the challenges your teen offers, check out IDEA 52, *Waving or Drowning?*, for some soothing tips.

Try another idea…

**'Sexuality – strong and warm and wild and free
Sexuality – your laws do not apply to me
Sexuality – come eat and drink and sleep with me
Sexuality – we can be what we want to be'**
Billy Bragg, lyrics from 'Sexuality'

Defining idea…

87

How did it go?

Q **I want to make sure my teen is aware of STIs and contraception – but I want to make sure my information is up to date! Where can I go to find youth friendly information? I don't want to offer him cold, clinical information.**

A *Your doctor's surgery will have up to date leaflets and information; alternatively, look in the phone book for a local specific youth health agency or clinic. Online, look at the fun but informative 'Like it is' website for young people at http://www.likeitis.org/contraception.html.*

Q **My 15-year-old daughter has become pregnant after having sex with her boyfriend who is also 15. Obviously I am stunned – and a little angry that she has acted so stupidly. What can I do to help her?**

A *She needs your support right now in whatever decisions she makes. Be careful to stay calm and do not express your anger; she will already know exactly how you feel. Concentrate on showing her your love and support. Although you can help her consider her options, she is the person who has to live with her decision. As a first step, consult your GP. This gives you access to appropriate healthcare for her needs whether she keeps the baby or has an abortion.*

Some services, such as Brook (http://www.brook.org.uk/), Planned Parenthood Federation (http://www.plannedparenthood.org/pp2/portal/)or Marie Stopes International (http://www.mariestopes.org.uk/) have counsellors who will be able to help her to explore how she feels about her pregnancy and give her impartial information on her options. Make sure she does not make any rash decisions she may come to regret later.

21

A fine romance?

It feels odd when your child first brings home a partner, but he may well fall deeply in love, developing a strong emotional and sexual bond with his partner.

Dismiss it as 'puppy love' at your peril!

Do you remember your first love? Most of us do, with affection – and some of us even marry them! I had an amazing thought as I started to write this chapter. I have been in love with four men in my life time – and I had met them all by the time I was 18! (I married my college sweetheart.) Each relationship, despite the fact that I was very young in each case, was deep and meaningful, and I loved the young men dearly. I still keep in touch with one of them personally; the other two still visit my parents. I remember the way I felt during our relationships, and this helps me to think about the deep well of emotions and passion that can be felt by teenagers – including yours and mine.

It is one thing inviting your teenage son's partner over for dinner, or to watch TV, but how do you cope if he wants a 'grown up sleepover'? I think your reaction depends on his age. You cannot condone under-age sex; it is illegal and fraught with complications for everyone involved. If your son (*or* daughter) is 18 or 19, you may think differently, however. Whether you like it or not, he is having sex. If you ban it under your roof, he will go elsewhere. If you do not feel comfortable with the situation, say so. But even if you do accept it, you do not have to issue carte blanche. Talk to him, and lay some ground rules, such as don't come down to breakfast in dressing gowns; no heavy snogging or innuendo in front of younger siblings – whatever will make you feel comfortable. Make it clear that your decision, if you have accepted a partner staying over, is for this *particular* partner, as you feel comfortable with this person sleeping in your house; if it should occur in future another decision will have to be made.

BREAKING UP IS HARD TO DO …

Here's an idea for you…

Show your teenage daughter photos of your own ex boy/girlfriends. This will offer a sense of perspective, as you talk about how much you loved them, but for one reason or another, the relationship stopped working. The photos will give your daughter a great laugh too, as they see the assortment of oddbods you declared your undying love to at one time or another … and that might cheer her up!

Relationship breakdowns can be extremely traumatic for your teen and his partner. Take it seriously. If he is the person being dumped, he may feel that the world is coming to an end. Be patient.

Even if he is the 'dumper' rather than the 'dumpee', things can still be emotionally fraught. This is especially true of a partner who has become part of the family and has made a relationship with you.

HEAVEN KNOWS, I'M MISERABLE NOW …

Whilst your teen is in the middle of a break up, keep an eye open for any signs of depression. He may want to stay at home more – which is fine up to a point, but encourage him to go out with friends, not only to take his mind off things, but also to get back 'in the swim.' Encourage him to talk about the break up if he wants – teenage friends soon get sick of listening to relationship woes! Let him know that overwork – perhaps burying himself in coursework or revision – is only a temporary solution, and the hurt feelings will still be there, waiting to be dealt with, when he re-emerges.

If your daughter is in the throes of a passionate affair, stand by with a listening ear. She may need help and advice. Check out IDEA 14, *Making time*, to find ways to connect.

Try another idea…

Your son may suffer a variety of physical symptoms after a break up too, such as loss of appetite, insomnia, nightmares, and even skin breakouts due to stress (just to add insult to injury).

Be optimistic when you talk to him about his feelings. Just make sure you don't say 'there are plenty more fish in the sea'; if it is *this* fish that he wanted, it won't help. Instead, pamper and praise your son, letting him know he is wonderful and that many people love him now – and will do in the future.

'Ah! A jumped-up pantry boy Who never knew his place He said "return the ring" He knows so much about these things …'
    THE SMITHS, 'This Charming Man'

Defining idea…

How did it go?

Q **My teenage son has just been dumped and seems very down. What can I do to cheer him up?**

A *He may be feeling rather unlovable and unattractive, so plenty of hugs are in order, plus a morale-boosting trip out. New clothes will help him feel better about himself, and he may fancy a new haircut or some other self care treat.*

Q **My daughter broke up with her boyfriend who had become part of the family – we have known him for two years. He still seems to want to hang around – he is friends with our son, and we like him too – but our daughter feels uncomfortable. What should I do?**

A *Your priority is your daughter. If she feels as though she is being stalked in her own house she will not thank you! Talk to her about it, and see if you can come to a compromise. Perhaps she would feel OK about him popping in through the day but would prefer that he did not hang around the house in the evenings. She may find it difficult at first, but if the boy agrees not to follow her round or make puppy dog eyes at her every time she looks up (and believe me, this happens!) she may be able to get used to it. It is valuable life lesson anyway; she needs to learn that a break up does not have to mean all out warfare!*

22

In with the in crowd?

Once your child becomes a teenager, you are no longer at the centre of her world. Now, her friends are her pivotal point of reference.

But what happens if those friends are what you see as a bad influence?

Separating from you as parents is a normal stage in your teenager's development. Once she has successfully launched herself out into the world, she will be happy to draw back close to you again, but she has to feel independent first. Part of that independence is expressed by building a friendship group.

She will want at some point – if not need – to be accepted by a peer group. She is moving away from the family but is feeling uncertain of her place in the world. A peer group offers alternatives to the family. She may adopt weird fashions and attitudes as she tries to fit in. Ride it out; it will pass. The danger comes when negative peer pressure encourages her to experiment with risk taking behaviour. It may be that her friends drink heavily, or take illegal drugs. It can seem that despite being brought up with certain moral values, your teenager is rejecting and abandoning them in favour of the 'one size fits all' moral mores of her group – and to a concerned parent, that can feel like rejection.

Here's an idea for you... **Help your teen to widen his friendship group. Encourage him to join an interest group linked to a hobby or sport where he may meet people with similar outlook on life. A part time job may also offer a new source of friends. Help him to investigate how to get involved in volunteer work in an area that interests him such as with a conservation group. Check out http://kidshealth.org/teen/school_jobs/jobs/volunteering.html to find out more.**

Try to understand the pressure she is under for a moment. Despite paying lip service to the idea that she is an individual, your daughter is at a stage in her life when she is desperate to fit in – just not with mainstream society. She needs to feel that she belongs to a group of her own.

It takes a brave teenager to stand against the flow of the stream, and it can lead to teasing and name calling – even to the point of bullying. All you can do is keep supporting her; validate her individuality and help her to 'stick to her guns'.

DON'T JUDGE TOO SOON

If you aren't keen on your teenager's friends, stop for a minute and consider why this is the case. Is it a symptom of your own baggage? Did the 'cool kids' look down on you when you were a teenager because you were a brainy 'boffin' or geek? Were you a Byronesque proto-goth, so you shunned the 'metal heads' as barely better than Neanderthals? The point is, don't let your erstwhile teenage prejudices turn you against your teenager's friendship group. Give them a chance. 'Buzz', under all that hair and grunge, may be an A student; the girl in the frightening Lolita-wear may be the most chaste of the group. Look beyond the trappings, make up and improbably placed piercings; other parents may find *your* little angel rather menacing!

Another thing to think about is this: we all have friends for different contexts. Apart from one or two 'multipurpose' best friends, we see different people to fulfil different functions in our lives. Some friends are great at providing support when we need it. Others are seemingly purely for 'entertainment' value. They

If your teen is lonely and depressed, find ways to help in IDEA 51, *Nobody understands me ...*

Try another idea...

are great fun to be with, but perhaps are unreliable or unable to keep confidences. It is the same for your teenager. Your daughter's new friend might seem vacuous, but she might offer something your daughter needs right now – perhaps the girl admires your daughter and makes her feel good about herself. And of course, remember that even cheerleaders can have hidden depths!

HOME ALONE? COPING WITH SOCIAL ISOLATION

Some teenagers make friends easily; others don't. Some are happy with few friends, but isolation can be devastating for a teenager, so be there to help your child. Stress that she is facing a common challenge – she may feel that everyone else is out having a great time except her – but this is not the case. Do not deny her hurt, but try to be objective and put the situation into context for her. Boost your teenager's self esteem, which may be feeling battered if she is feeling left out. Give her positive reinforcement to help to build her confidence. Tell her she is pretty, clever, talented etc. This in turn will help her to make friends more easily as she projects a happier, likeable persona.

'You can make more friends in two months by becoming interested in other people than you can in two years by trying to get other people interested in you.'
DALE CARNEGIE, motivational speaker and author of *How to Win Friends and Influence People* (1936)

Defining idea...

Q **My teenager doesn't bring his friends home any more, preferring to go to their houses. How can I let him know they are welcome?**

A   *It may be that your son is afraid you will be too judgmental. Think hard – do you ridicule young people with extreme haircuts/make up/clothes in his presence, even in jest? Let him know that you will do your best not to embarrass him if he brings friends round, and let him know they are welcome. Suggest friends come round and provide snacks – and your absence! Don't hover – you may be putting him off because you are too keen to be involved!*

Q **How can I help my child to withstand negative peer pressure, such as 'everyone else is having sex ...'?**

A   *Strong support from family can help teenagers get pressure into perspective. Older siblings can be especially helpful; firstly, they are not you! Secondly, they have experienced similar pressures in recent times. The more confident your child is, the easier he will find resisting being sucked in to activities he doesn't really want to take part in.*

23

Rainbow youth: when your teen is gay

During adolescence many boys and girls have same-sex crushes and experiences, but are not lesbian or gay.

Other adolescents, though, may come to understand that they have felt 'different' all their lives, but come to an awareness of their gay or bisexual orientation during their teens.

You may find it difficult to come to terms with the fact your child is a sexual being, let alone gay, and possibly different to you if you are straight. You may experience feelings of loss as the child you thought you had is replaced by the child you actually have. The first and most important lesson for you to learn is this: your gay teenager is the same person he always was. He is the same child you cuddled, nursed, played with and loved. That doesn't change because your teenager is gay. The second lesson is this: your teenager didn't *choose* to be gay. He was made that way,

Here's an idea for you… **Your teenage child may have been denying her feelings for a long time, maybe years. That takes a great deal of emotional energy. She may have tried to use alcohol or other drugs to numb the feelings. She may even have been depressed enough to have considered suicide. When you find this out it can rock your world. Encourage your child to talk to you, but be prepared to find out things about experiences she has had that will make your ears bleed as you imagine the pain she has been through. Be accepting and offer lots of hugs. Your child has been hurt and needs comfort. Encourage her to seek contact with a gay youth organisations such as Rainbow Youth (http:// www.rainbowyouth.org. nz/) Gay Youth UK (http:// www.gayyouthuk.org.uk/) OutProud (http://www. outproud.org/).**

and that is not going to change, so get used to it. He did *not* decide to be gay to spite you; he did *not* 'turn out gay' because of anything you did or didn't do as parents. Accept these truths and you will find it easier to adjust.

If you think you are finding it difficult to adjust to your child's identity as a gay person, stop to think for a moment. He is having an even harder time of it. Society is very negative about gay people. Ridiculous stereotypes and idiotic ideas are circulated about gay people in the media and in everyday conversations. Many men feel uncomfortable around gay men because they are afraid of sexual advances and contact. Firstly, they should not presume they are so gorgeous that a gay man couldn't resist making a proposition; secondly – they are buying into the stereotype that gay men are always on the prowl, looking for sexual encounters. Like heterosexual men, gay men have many facets to their lives, sex being only a part of that.

Girls who come to realise they are lesbians face stereotypes – that they are all aggressive *uber-dykes*; they have flat top haircuts and wear Dr Martens – or, they face a salacious fascination from men with sexual fantasies about lipstick lesbians performing for their pleasure.

Gay youths face bullying in school and even violence as a result of their sexuality. In a study of lesbian and gay youth in New York City, 41% reported attacks from family members, peers, or strangers.

HOW CAN I HELP MY TEEN?

- Read about being gay – both of you. You can get books from the library, and from most bookshops. Be careful – not all reading is supportive and especially older (or religiously motivated) books may suggest that gay sexuality can (and should) be altered; they may even suggest that being gay is a mental illness. This is all rubbish born out of fear of the unknown.

Try another idea…

Let your teen know you love and accept her for herself. Check out IDEA 30, *Positive Parenting: The power of praise*, for ideas on how to let her know how you feel.

Defining idea…

'Be who you are and say what you feel, because those who mind don't matter and those who matter don't mind.'
DR SEUSS

99

- Websites can also be really useful, both as a source of information and as a point of contact for your teenager to access helplines and gay counsellors who can help him to deal with his feelings at this time.
- Is there a gay person you know who your child can talk to? This may be a relative or friend of the family who can help your teenager come to terms with his identity as a gay person. We all need role models!
- Your child may need a great deal of support to 'come out' to people, especially peers. He will need a great deal of support from you as he may face a lot of negative and even hostile reactions. Don't force the issue – he may want to pop in and out of the closet for some time, perhaps telling close family or friends first before having the confidence to tell the world.

Q **Our son has just told us he is gay. I think my husband is in denial as he refuses to talk about it at all. He says 'It's just a phase'. I need to talk about my feelings, so what can I do?**

How did it go?

A *Denial may take many forms: ignoring the situation, hostility, or rejection. Your husband may just be taking longer to adjust than you – the parent who is the same sex as the gay child often finds this harder.*

  When your husband seems relaxed, gently raise the subject again. Personalise what you say – tell your husband he is a great father, and that your son needs him now more than ever. You may also find it helps you to talk to an organisation that helps the parents of gay children to understand a little more about their child's sexuality, and their own feelings of confusion.

Q **I'd like to read some books to help me understand more about my daughter's sexuality, and make sure she has plenty of informative reading material. Can you recommend any books?**

A *Try* Straight Parents, Gay Children: Keeping Families Together *by Robert A. Bernstein (ISBN 1560254521). Look at the website http://www.pinkbooks. com/ to find a great range of recommended reading.*

24

Rules of the house

There is no magic 'fix it' to make living with teenagers smooth and easy.

But agreeing to a few house rules can help your teenager to adopt responsible behaviour that will be of benefit to her throughout her life.

There is nothing wrong with rules per se – whatever your daugher thinks! We are subject to rules in every part of our lives – legal rules, workplace rules, society's rules – so why not family rules? As long as they are fair, rules help to make organisations work smoothly, and protect members – and that includes families. If family rules are created organically, growing out of the needs of family members and in the interests of keeping family members safe and cared for, your teenager should agree to keep to them.

That's the theory, anyway! It doesn't always work that way with teenagers, but it's a good starting point. House rules should not be imposed suddenly, but should evolve out of the rules established when your teenage children were younger. Agreed rules enable groups of people to co-operate and live together. If your teen-age daughter understands the reasons behind the rules, although she is hormo-

Here's an idea for you… **If you have rules, you need sanctions for when the rules are broken. Reasonable consequences should ideally be tied in to the infraction e.g. using the phone repeatedly for chats during peak cost tariff time, despite being asked not to, could lead to not being able to use the telephone for a period. Not calling home to let you know he is going to be later than expected could lead to not being allowed out the next weekend etc.**

nally programmed to push against them, she is more likely to accept them. Talking to her about the principles and values behind your rules will help to guide your child as she moves towards independent life outside of the family.

Rules must be adaptable, and applied in a way that is suited to the age of your children. Rules need to be relaxed as your child's independence and competence grows; new rules will be needed to address new situations such as going out in the evening with friends, or staying home while you go away on holiday.

Be careful not to impose too many rules. Decide what really matters, and let the small irritations drop. I try to remind myself what it was like sharing a house when I was a student – and at least *try* to act accordingly. I expect my teenagers to put away their stuff (it doesn't always happen though!) but I wouldn't pompously say 'The rule is, you put away your own stuff'; I would say, 'I need to hoover, so you need to clear your things away.' Be flexible – for example, you might be prepared to tolerate your daughter's preferences for tidiness within her own room (i.e. none) but not in shared areas of the house.

Some people like to use family conferences or meetings to negotiate house rules. That is too formal for our house, but might work for you. I would rather talk about things over dinner than call a meeting. As long as everyone is heard, and no one pulls rank just because they *can*, either approach works. Only *you* know what works best for *your* family.

If the rules keep getting broken, check out IDEA 25, *Crime and punishment*, for suggested sanctions.

Try another idea…

RULES TO THINK ABOUT ADOPTING

- *Parents have the responsibility to keep their children safe*. Teenagers tend to oppose parental rules that seem arbitrary, but are more likely to grudgingly accept rules that are designed to keep them safe. Curfews are widely disputed, but the concept itself is usually accepted because it is meant to keep your child safe.
- *Everyone has the right to live in a welcoming, comfortable home*. This covers putting away the items teenagers seem programmed to drop in hallways, bathrooms etc. It also covers playing loud music at inconvenient times (but not all the time – some folks find loud music pleasurable … and that is bound to include your daughter) etc.
- *Everyone has to pitch in and help*. Everyone, including younger children and teenagers, needs to help with housework and chores – dishes, sorting laundry etc. Above all, make sure things are done fairly and no one is expected to do a larger share because they are older – or heaven forbid, a *girl*.
- *Everyone has a right to their own space*. If your teenager has her own room, allow her to decorate it as she wishes, and leave it as messy or neat as she chooses – as long as she does not expect anyone to go in there and clean. This needs qualifiers though – you should insist your child brings down crockery unless you want it all to disappear (and when you search for it, it will appear to have a science experiment growing inside). If your child does not bring down laundry, it doesn't get washed and she takes over her own laundry etc.

'Parents were invented to make children happy by giving them something to ignore.'
OGDEN NASH

Defining idea…

105

How did
it go?

Q **My 16-year-old daughter has finished her exams and is off school for the summer. She listens to loud music in her room after we have gone to bed. We have asked her many times to stop, but she does it night after night. What can we do?**

A *Your daughter is being very unreasonable. She may be able to lie in but you have to be up for work and need a good night's sleep. Explain this to her firmly and calmly. Tell her that if the disturbances do not stop she will not be allowed to listen to music after a curfew of 10pm.*

Q **My 17-year-old son brings his friends home, which is great – but they leave snack wrappers on the floor, and smoke in the living room (which we don't allow). Is it reasonable for me to object?**

A *Make your son's friends feel welcome, but clarify your ground rules with your son in private. It is your house, and you should feel comfortable there. Give your son the option: either he makes sure the wrappers etc. are thrown away and the 'no smoking' rule is enforced or you will. He is likely to find that rather embarrassing ... Do not put up with unreasonable behaviour and insist that the 'rules of the house' are adhered to. It is likely that your son's friends are just being thoughtless, rather than unpleasant, so a gentle reminder should work.*

25

Crime and punishment

When a child is small and wilfully does something wrong, you punish him. You might ban treats, or send him to his room.

But what can you do when your teenager behaves badly?

If your teenager is to stay safe and healthy, there will be times when you need to back up your house rules with sanctions. Without sanctions, rules can turn into empty threats. Sanctions – or that highly value loaded and perhaps outmoded word 'discipline' – will help your child to develop self-control. Discipline helps to define boundaries of acceptable behaviour and helps to accustom your teenager to the idea that there are consequences for breaching them.

When a child crayons on the wallpaper or pulls the cat's tail, you know how to respond. You explain why the action was wrong, and impose a 'punishment' that fits the crime and rectifies the problem – cleaning off the crayon; feeding the cat for a week. With teenagers, everything is less clear cut, and that makes life hard for parents wanting to do the best for their child.

Here's an idea for you...

Develop the ability to know when to back off. This can be done by telling your daughter that you are tired of going over the same ground time and again – perhaps about healthy eating, for example. Tell her you have had enough of making meals that are left uneaten. Say you know she feels nagged, so you are turning over the responsibility to her. You will stock the fridge, freezer and fruit bowl etc. and she is welcome to join the family for meals but she will have to 'contract in' i.e. find out what you are cooking and ask for a portion. If she doesn't want it, she can make herself something.

The principle stays the same. You need, as calmly as possible, to explain why the action was wrong – it may have hurt or inconvenienced someone, for example, or property may have been destroyed, which will cost money to replace. Then you need to think together about putting things right.

Think carefully about what punishment is for. If it is not designed to make your teen think about why his actions were wrong and the effect it had on others, it is unlikely to work and can turn into a power trip. Your teen will use his energy to feel angry towards you instead of thinking about why his actions were wrong and how to make reparations.

The punishment you decide to impose should help your teenager to connect his actions with the consequences of those actions. If that is achieved, a punishment is successful, as consequences are something teenagers find very hard to understand.

Carefully choose a few principles for your 'family rules', concentrating on the most important issues such as policies on alcohol, curfew, and how your teenager should consider the needs and feelings of other family members. If you have too many rules – especially petty ones – he is bound to rebel. Once again, consider the mantra 'remember what is important'; if you are constantly punishing your child for small infractions, the impact will wear off and he may become distant.

Are you regularly at loggerheads with your teenager? Read IDEA 9, *Fight club: how to avoid arguments, and de-escalation tactics*, for ways of taking the heat out of a situation.

Try another idea…

HAVE CLEAR EXPECTATIONS

Your teenager needs to know what is expected of him. Otherwise, he does not have a chance of avoiding sanctions! Giving him clear guidelines, preferably after formulating house rules together, will help to keep him on the 'straight and narrow'. Boundaries will help him feel secure, as he will know what is expected. Your expectations of his behaviour should be high but not unreasonable, or he will constantly feel that he does not quite 'measure up'.

'If you want to recapture your youth, just cut off his allowance.'

RED BUTTONS

Defining idea…

109

Be very clear about what the consequences will be for breaking rules, without being dictatorial in advance! Let him know that habitual lateness means that he is not being responsible; if he is not responsible enough to be organised and get on the bus as agreed, then he is not responsible and mature enough to be out on his own at night. Be flexible though – for example, if curfew is 11pm and your child is a little late (say 10 minutes) that is one thing; if he rings ahead and lets you know, he is being responsible and should be praised for his behaviour. If he rings to let you know the bus has not turned up but he will be on the next one that arrives, once again, he is being responsible. When he gets home, praise him but let him know that being late was the exception and he should not make a habit of it because he was given some leeway this time. Otherwise, he may get lax about getting to the bus stop on time because the excuse 'I missed the bus' worked last time …

Q **My husband and I parent by different rules. He thinks I am too laid back but I think he nags the kids too much. I want to present a united front, but how can we compromise?**

How did it go?

A *Talk about what you agree upon first – there will be some common ground! This helps to set a cooperative mood. Then think about the difficult issues. You could make a list and work through them. Perhaps untidiness is getting your husband down, and he thinks the kids should help more. He may be over reacting, but if it upsets him, some compromise needs to be reached. Perhaps he could stand their rooms being a bit of a mess as long as the rest of the house is kept clear of piles of clothes, CDs etc. Alternatively, suggest keeping a box for each of your teenage children where dumped items are put and tell your kids to empty their boxes into their rooms at night.*

Q **My 14-year-old does not complete homework, and I get letters from school complaining. What can I do?**

A *Talk to her about the reasons for not completing work – is it too hard? Does she understand? If not, encourage her to ask her teacher to explain. Is she having trouble organising her time? Help her to make a realistic home-work timetable. If she is just being a bit lazy, impose sanctions such as no TV, PC or going out with friends until her homework is completed.*

26

What the f*ck?!

It's one thing when your teenage daughter swears in the company of her friends – but another thing entirely when she swears at home – especially when it is aimed at you!

Swearing and cursing — what is acceptable in your house, and how can you change bad habits?

Teenagers swear for a variety of reasons; some are the same as the reasons why adults swear. It vents frustration in a most satisfying manner! You may feel that cursing is OK in certain contexts, but less so if your teenager releases a stream of invective at a family gathering, in front of younger siblings and causing granny to choke on her sherry.

Teenage children swear for many reasons. They may swear to make themselves feel more 'adult' – particularly if they hear you swear, and think it's what adults do. They may also have picked up cursing as a legitimate way of communicating via the media, particularly TV and films, and if a favourite star or role model swears regularly. Geoffrey Hughes, author of *Swearing: A Social History of Foul Language, Oaths and Profanity in English*, says that 'The influence of Hollywood has become a dominant

Make sure you consistently show your teenager that there are consequences attached to his actions. Challenge his foul language directly, firmly and calmly. Tell him you are unhappy about it. Say that although you are not happy about it, you understand that it is his choice whether he swears when he is with his friends. Impress upon him the idea that it is *your* choice what sort of language is acceptable in the house, where you and other family members have to hear it. If necessary, add firm and consistent sanctions so your child knows what will happen if he continues to use foul language. That may be refusing to give pocket money, not allowing him to use the phone; etc.

factor [in the shift in attitudes towards swearing], initially for restraint, but subsequently for license.'

Your teenager may also swear to get attention – even if it is negative. If swearing gets an immediate reaction from you, she will do it to make sure you listen. She may swear to rebel, and to make a statement about her independence – to let you know you are no longer in control of her. Of course, she may swear to look 'cool' in front of her peers. Using bad language may just be another way of trying to fit in.

Only you know how much cursing and swearing is acceptable in your house, and you need to think carefully and be consistent. Some people find any foul language abhorrent; others find it acceptable in certain circumstances and in certain company. Set a standard, and keep to it – applying the standard to yourself as well as your teenagers.

HOW TO DEAL WITH IT

■　*Talk about the words.* Talk about why people swear. What words are 'swear' words? What do they mean? You can make swearing sound stupid if you reduce the foul word to its functional (often biological!) meaning. Telling someone to 'intercourse off' is not quite as satisfying as its Anglo Saxon alternative, but it's not as offensive either ...

- *Set limits.* Explain why and when foul language is not acceptable in your family. Be careful not to be hypocritical. If you swear when you hit your fingers with a hammer during a DIY spree, you cannot justly condemn your teen for swearing when she hurts herself. Talk about when it is absolutely not acceptable to swear i.e. in front of younger children, grandparents etc.

- *Consider alternatives.* Some teenagers (and adults!) have a hard time expressing angry feelings. Swearing is often the result of frustration. Legitimise your teenager's anger, telling her that it's OK to be angry with you, but there are certain ways of expressing that anger that are not acceptable.

   If she stomps off to her room, don't call her back; let her go until she is calm. We all feel like stomping off sometimes! It's a healthy way for her to express her anger. If your child curses at you, tell her it is not acceptable. But if you take this tack, make sure you never swear at her. Teens smell hypocrisy a mile off.

- *Be positive.* Sometimes, your teenager will be angry and handle her feelings well. She may tell you how mad she is without swearing – although she'll slam doors and flounce. Once things are calm again, make sure you acknowledge her behaviour. Tell her it was mature behaviour and you were impressed.

If your teenager shows a lack of respect, could it be the case that you are guilty of the same? Read IDEA 28, *R.E.S.P.E.C.T.!*, to find out more.

Try another idea…

'There ought to be a room in every house to swear in. It's dangerous to have to repress an emotion like that.'

MARK TWAIN

Defining idea…

115

How did it go?

Q **My son says I am being too uptight about swearing because I do not tolerate it in the house. I do not swear and I hate to hear foul language. Should I do what he says, and 'loosen up'?**

A *Your son may be among people who swear frequently; he may choose to join in whilst he is in their company. However, he has to understand that swearing makes you uncomfortable and you have a right to ban it in your home. Explain this to him calmly – and remember, it doesn't matter what everyone else is doing; you have to do what is right for your family – and that includes you!*

Q **Things have got really bad at home, with my 17-year-old son swearing at me and calling me a bitch when we argue. I just don't know what to do – I feel really hurt. Is there any way of changing his awful behaviour?**

A *Your son's behaviour is completely unacceptable, and you need to make him understand this. Raise the subject when you are both calm. Tell him how hurt it makes you feel, and that you take the insults personally. Ask him how he would feel if someone else was abusive to you – perhaps one of his friends. Assert yourself. You have the right to be treated with respect, especially in your own home.*

27

Manners! Does your teen have a rude 'tude?

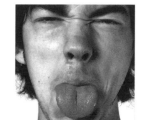

The very word 'manners' sounds almost archaic. Many of the petty rules about which fork to use, or where to place a glass on the table, are outdated.

But when 'manners' means knowing what behaviour is appropriate, and respect for self and others, they are needed as much today as ever.

Good manners are noticeable. When you are treated with courtesy instead of rudeness, it makes you feel good about yourself. You feel respected and valued. When you were a child, your parents probably emphasised good manners that may seem outmoded today – and some are. We must help today's children understand that they are not in this world alone and that everyone matters. Our children's future and success will be enhanced by the use of appropriate behaviour.

Daily, you see bad manners exhibited in the workplace, on the roads, in shops – it seems that rudeness has become a performance art. However, teaching your teens about manners helps to make your own small part of the world – your family and social circle – a better place to be.

By 'manners' I do not mean formal behaviour such as how to use cutlery in an expensive restaurant; I mean behaving in a manner that is thoughtful and kind, and considers the feelings of the people around you. Your teenager needs to understand why manners are important – he will not just adopt them because it is 'polite'! Manners are an expression of respect and consideration for others. Knowing how to act appropriately in public, and learning to say *please* and *thank you* are social skills your teenager needs to develop into a mature and thoughtful adult.

Here's an idea for you...

For a fun look at modern manners – from the *How Rude!* series – check out *The Teenagers' Guide to Good Manners, Proper Behaviour, and Not Grossing People Out'* by Alex J. Packer. It covers everything from 'Toiletiquette' (polite bathroom sharing) to 'Netiquette' (cyberspace behaviour codes). It will make your teenager laugh – and she just might absorb something along the way ...

Bad manners are prevalent in schools. Teenagers may treat their peers badly, teasing them and making cruel jibes about people's looks, clothes, sexuality and 'popularity'. Try walking round a large school as lessons change from one to another and you may well see pushing and shoving, doors dropped in people's faces – it can be quite threatening! Better schools which take a holistic approach to education to care for the 'whole child' make manners a priority and politeness becomes part of the school ethos, reinforced by rules such as keeping to the side, moving round the school in a particular direction, holding doors etc. It makes lesson changes calmer and less threatening to younger or nervous students, and bad behaviour flashpoints are avoided. Many schools complain about the manners of their students, but some of the teachers fail to treat their charges – and each other – with courtesy and respect. If a teacher belittles your teenager, or treats him without respect, your child is learning a lesson – but not a positive one.

Does your teen's lack of manners include bad language? Read IDEA 26, What the F*ck?!, to find solutions.

Try another idea...

Teenagers, like younger children, learn from watching the behaviour of others. If the adults around them behave rudely, or are unfair and selfish, they will learn from that model. Here's the hard part – you are their greatest role model. As a society, we have allowed our own manners to slip, so it is no wonder that our children are behaving disrespectfully. We are reaping what we have sown.

Quite apart from the cultural value of good manners, they will help your teenager to get on in life. People with good manners are nice to be around. They are more likely to be popular and form good strong relationships with others as they make people feel good about themselves. If your teenager learns to act with consideration and politeness and knows how to act in all kinds of situations, his confidence will soar. Employers and college professors will see polite teenagers as more mature than their counterparts, and this can only help your teenager in a competitive world.

'Manners are a sensitive awareness of the feelings of others. If you have that awareness, you have good manners, no matter what fork you use.'
EMILY POST, American authority on social behaviour 1872–1960

Defining idea...

How did
it go?

Q **My daughter has dreadful table manners, despite being taught from an early age how to act correctly. We went out to dinner at a restaurant the other night and I was embarrassed by her behaviour as she slouched on the table, scooping food up like a power shovel – it was awful. I don't want to hurt her feelings, but what can I do?**

A *This is common – and usually passes in time! It may be that your daughter is rebelling – rejecting your values because she knows it pushes your buttons. It may be that she has become used to eating on a tray in front of the television and has gotten out of the habit of eating together, politely, at the table. She may need a quick 'refresher course'. Whenever family schedules allow, try to eat together at the table and model good manners. Don't get het up about her seeming lack of manners or it will cause tension – and in the scheme of things, her table manners are not such a calamity!*

Q **My teenagers laugh when I remind them about good manners – they say it doesn't matter these days. What can I say to convince them otherwise?**

A *You can try to persuade them by reminding them of the values that lie behind manners – kindness, respect and consideration. It won't hurt to remind them that good manners will make them stand out from the crowd favourably when they are trying to make a good impression, such as at college interviews, with the parents of boyfriends and girlfriends etc. – and that makes life easier!*

28

R.E.S.P.E.C.T.!

If someone asked you if you respect your teenage daughter, the answer would probably be yes. But does she know that?

If the subject of 'respect' is brought up, when discussing parenting teenagers, it is likely that people would discuss the lack of respect they feel they are getting from their teenagers. But why should we expect to be respected if we do not show them we respect them as people in return?

To respect someone means to admire them and hold them in high esteem. If you respect someone, you care about what they think; you take their wishes and views into account when making decisions. Can you honestly say that this is how you treat your teenager?

It is easy to treat your children with less than respect – you get into a spiral where they are rude to you, so you bark orders at them ('Tidy your room!') rather than

Here's an idea for you...

Make a list of the qualities you admire in your teenager – and keep it handy. It is especially useful to read during the challenging moments of parenting teenagers that will inevitably arrive! Which qualities do you respect in him? It could be many things, such as his loving nature, honesty, perseverance or humour. Tell him what you respect about him. 'I really respect the way you worked so hard on that essay, even though you found it hard. It showed real perseverance' or 'I really respect the way you stood up to your classmates when they were teasing you – it was really brave.' Remember, you are looking for qualities, rather than achievements.

make polite requests ('Could you have a sort out in your room and bring down any dirty washing please?'). Then they respond in kind, and the cycle begins again.

It is possible to break this cycle. A relationship built on mutual respect is more fulfilling for everyone concerned – both you and your teenager – and developing this type of relationship will help you to make a transition when the time comes to the relationship you will have with your adult child.

To truly respect your child is to admire her for who she is – right now. If you do not treat your child with respect, how will she develop self respect? If you, as a parent, do not model 'respectful' behaviour towards your teenager, how can you hope to get it in turn?

THE POWER OF POSITIVE COMMUNICATION

The way in which you talk to your teenager reveals a great deal about how much you respect her. Respecting her means you will listen carefully to what she says and not be half distracted by chores, TV programmes or thoughts of work. She needs your full attention. Don't forget to ask her about her day – and encourage her to ask about yours in return. These seemingly simple conversations are what keep you in touch with the daily life of your teenager.

You should talk to your teenager honestly and include her in family discussions appropriate to her age. If you are thinking of moving, for example, you should discuss her feelings at the earliest opportunity. Teenagers must be involved in family decision making if they are to feel that their views and feelings are respected.

Are you finding it hard to communicate with your teenager? Check out IDEA 8, *Learning to listen: how to open channels of communication*, for ways to solve the problem.

Try another idea…

You should aim to create a respectful climate where you and your teenage child can share thoughts and feelings – including negative ones – without fear of rejection and aggression. If you achieve this, you will be more easily able to solve problems and conflicts without full scale rows. Treating your teenager in this way gives her a blueprint for developing satisfying adult relationships with friends, co-workers and lovers.

Families are made up of collections of individuals – our children all have very different personalities, despite incredibly similar upbringing! Think about your own family – either your children or your siblings – and you will have a picture of the variety that may be found within one family! It is not surprising that these individuals, even though bound together by family ties, have very different opinions and varying likes and dislikes. In a family that values individuality, family members are treated with respect whatever their views. Show your teenager that you respect her individuality by taking an interest in her hobbies and enthusiasms. Make sure, for instance, that you attend any concerts or exhibitions your teenager takes part in to show her how important she is to you.

'A youth is to be regarded with respect. How do you know that his future will not be equal to our present?'
CONFUCIUS

Defining idea…

123

Q **My teenage son says I do not respect his privacy. I clean his room and never pry but this seems to be a bone of contention. He doesn't like his younger brother going into his room when he is not there either. How can I improve matters?**

A   *Firstly, stop cleaning his room. Give him a small lidded plastic box with his own cleaning supplies, plus rubbish sacks, and say that as long as he keeps his room in a reasonable state you will not interfere.*

    Think about knocking before you enter his room, or perhaps calling out 'Hi there – can I come in?' as you enter the room. This may make him feel you are respecting his privacy more. Consider fitting a lock to his room so he can lock his brother out of it when he is not there.

Q **My son treats me with little respect, talking to me if I had some sort of terminal stupidity disease. Why should I bother myself about showing that I respect him?**

A   *Most teenagers can be found treating their parents like old duffers at some point – even parents treat their parents in this way at times! The thing is, though, he needs to have a role model. If you bark orders at him and treat him disrespectfully, he will model your behaviour and send your disrespect winging back to you. It is hard to break out of negative behaviour patterns but is worth it in the long run. At first you may feel a little disheartened, but over time your efforts will be rewarded.*

29

Little nagging problems

There is nothing more annoying than being continually nagged. Ask any teenager.

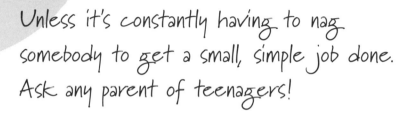

Unless it's constantly having to nag somebody to get a small, simple job done. Ask any parent of teenagers!

You know the scenario – you notice a couple of hours after dinner that the dishes aren't washed, and mention to your teenager that he should not forget to do them. 'Yes mum – I *know*' he grumbles.

An hour later, you notice the dishes are still there. 'Don't forget to do these dishes' you say, to be met with a sigh as he replies 'I said I'd do them … and I will.'

Later still, you wander through to make a cup of coffee and he is sat at the computer, chatting to friends. The dishes are still in a pile at the sink. 'The dishes are still there – you need to wash them', you say irritably. Your teenager rolls his eyes. 'They'll get done … stop nagging me!' he groans, not taking his eyes off the screen.

It is hard to stop nagging, because you get set into a negative pattern. Try to break out by taking some breathing space. Instead of launching into an all out nag attack, close the door on the dishes and take a walk round the block to calm yourself. Or go into another room and put on some music and lose yourself for a few moments. Giving yourself time to wind down will help you to be reasonable and will give you the emotional energy to approach the problem in a new way, instituting a new system that can avoid the need for nagging entirely!

Bedtime rolls round. Your son wanders off to his room and you lock up – only to find the dishes in a pile next to the sink. With much crashing about, you wash the dishes – you can't bear to come down to crusty dishes at breakfast time. You have spent the whole evening trying to get him to wash the dishes, to no avail. How can you stop wasting time in this way?

Basically, your teenager has decided he would rather put up with the drone of your nagging than do his chores. You have given him the message that you are not taking any action to back up your requests; in fact, you even do the chore for him!

When you remind, ask, cajole or nag a child about a chore but don't back up your requests with any action, he is very likely to make the choice that he would rather listen to your nagging than do the task.

MAKING CHANGES

You are going to have to get really proactive to change things. Your teenager is used to getting away with things, so changes may well come as a shock!

To avoid nagging – which is a soul sucking exercise – think hard about *exactly* what you want your child to do before you ask him to carry out a task. Clarity is everything. Be specific and do not make the task sound optional. Adding a time frame is useful – 'I want that job completed before we sit down to dinner, please.'

If the deadline for the task to be completed approaches, and your recalcitrant teenager shows no inclination to carry it out, remind him of the deadline. If the task is walking the dog, hand him the lead and say 'It's nearly dinner time – but you still have time to take the dog out if you go now.'

If you're tired of nagging, it could mean something is being lost in the translation. Read IDEA 14, *Making time*, to check for ways to make time to connect.

Try another idea…

'Naggers always know what they are doing. They weigh up the risks, then they go on and on and on until they get what they want or until they get punched.'

JOOLS HOLLAND, musician

Defining idea…

127

If the deadline is reached and the task is still not done, you need respond. You have several options. You can, for example, link a consequence to the chore that has not been carried out. That may be that they he is allowed to sit down to dinner until the task is done; or that he is not allowed to go round to a friend's house or the youth club after dinner as planned, as he has to stay and complete the chore he did not carry out before dinner.

You may decide to do the chore yourself – don't shoot me! – and tell your child that you have done his chore, because you could not wait any longer for it to be done. Since you did his chore, he has to make up for this by doing a different job for you – right now. Explain that he ate into your time by not carrying out the first task, so you need him to carry out another task to make up for it. Here's a tip – make the 'extra' chore something more arduous or less pleasant than the first task, and the lesson is more likely to be remembered.

If he continues to avoid chores, do not nag; instead, tell him you need to talk. Tell he that he is acting unfairly; you do not want to nag and it is a boring waste of time. Then talk about how things need to change, and ask him for suggestions.

Q   **I hear myself nag and hate it – I'm turning into my mother! How can I stop myself?**

How did it go?

A   *Listening to yourself makes you aware of what it is you are doing – so you are halfway there! Try to take a break – wander into the garden and calm yourself down. Then start the programme – institute a deadline, and back this up with sanctions. It will soon pay dividends!*

Q   **My daughter does not seem to avoid chores out of meanness; she just seems to genuinely forget. How can I help her?**

A   *Tell her that if she needs a reminder, she could set the alarm on her mobile phone organiser to remind herself, or she could keep a checklist taped to the fridge, ticking off tasks as they are carried out. Make sure, though, that 'I forgot' isn't just a stock answer, given to excuse the fact she has not done her chores.*

30

Positive parenting: the power of praise

We all need praise. We respond to positive feedback on our performance at work; we bask in compliments about our appearance. Teens need praise too!

Praise makes us all feel good and boosts our self esteem. It is even more crucial for the wellbeing of your teen who may be feeling insecure and inadequate.

Teenagers are often weighed down by the pressures of school work and from shifts and power struggles amongst their peers – and even their friends. Your daughter may be grumpy, moody and at times uncommunicative, but she needs your support and encouragement more than ever.

It's easy to hand out negative attention to your teenager – nagging to get jobs done; complaining about the state of her room; grumbling about curfews not adhered to – but it is too easy to forget to praise her!

Here's an idea for you...

If you are feeling negative and beaten down by arguments, you may feel you cannot think of anything to praise. Prepare yourself by sitting down and making a list of the things you like most about your child. It's not enough to love him – you need to think about the things you actually like. However difficult your teenager is being, there will be something! He may be well organised, friendly, or have a great sense of humour. The point is, you need to find areas to focus on to make yourself feel positive, so you can offer praise and encouragement.

Don't forget that, as with younger children, if you are not giving your teenager enough of your time you can reinforce antisocial and unhelpful behaviour when you notice it and 'validate' it with your attention. Remember the 'catch her being good' principle and 'notice' good behaviour when it happens and offer praise.

It is important to give encouragement in a genuine way, as your teenager will be able to sniff out phoney praise a mile off – even when given with the best intentions. Don't go *over the top,* and make sure you praise something specific. For example, if your daughter is normally quick to fight with her brother, but manages to hold back when he borrows her CDs without asking, you could praise her for her behaviour saying something along the lines of, 'Hey – that was great. I was really impressed when you didn't shout at your brother for his thoughtless behaviour.' Or if your son usually grunts at your friends when they telephone, but on one occasion he has a chat with your friend, asking after her family, work etc., praise him for that, saying something like, 'Thanks for asking about Frances' work; she is having a busy time recently and will really appreciate the effort.'

Notice and thank your teenager when she does a chore. Even though it is accepted that she has to do the task – whether it is walking the dog or washing the dishes – it is nice not to be taken for granted. Think about it; you may cook the dinner nearly every night and

Is your teenager struggling with low self esteem due to body image anxieties? Read IDEA 44, *A weighty issue*, for tips on changing things.

Try another idea...

it may be taken as a given that it is one of 'your' chores – but it still feels great to be thanked for making a lovely meal. It is the same for your children with their chores.

Make sure you notice if your teenager is putting in a lot of study time and trying harder than usual at school. We are quick enough to point out when our children are not studying enough – so the reverse should be true too. Incidentally, this raises an important point. Don't save praise for achievements – though they are of course worthy of praise. It is more important to praise attitude and effort. You need to find a way of offering praise and encouragement to your teenage children on a regular, everyday basis. If you tie them into the idea that praise is only given when they achieve great grades, it may increase the stress they already feel and put them under even more pressure.

If you are not used to giving praise and encouragement freely, you may find it difficult at first – particularly if you are having difficulties with your teenage child. But being positive and noticing even her small efforts could be enough to stop a downward negative spiral of behaviour in its tracks. Give it a go – you have everything to gain!

'There are high spots in all of our lives and most of them have come about through encouragement from someone else. I don't care how great, how famous or successful a man or woman may be, each hungers for applause.'

GEORGE M. ADAMS,
American author (1878–1962)

Defining idea...

133

How did it go?

Q **My mother always used to praise my brother and I with a back handed criticism of the other. She used to say that I was neat and tidy, for example, unlike my slobby brother. She used to tell him that he was clever at school but then laughed at my work saying 'at least you've got looks on your side!' I remember how it felt and don't want to do that to my kids. How can I make things different for them?**

A *A parent should never use praise of one child as a way of criticising another. It can set the children up to compete with each other in an unhealthy way; it also has far reaching effects on self image and esteem – as you know. Instead, praise your children separately – they are different people after all, and will be good at different things. Find small, seemingly inconsequential things to praise as well as big important achievements – such as helping you carry in the shopping from the car, or playing with a younger sibling. Incidentally, it may be worth gently confronting your mother about her skewed use of praise. She may not like it; she probably meant it with the best of intentions – but you need to be able to have your say so you can move on.*

Q **I'm worried that too much praise may make my son stop trying. Is this a real danger?**

A *No! Being praised encourages us to do better, not worse. There is more danger that an unpraised child will stop bothering because nobody recognises his efforts. Get encouraging!*

31
School sucks

Some adults, looking through rose-tinted glasses, see their school days as the best days of their lives.

For many teenagers, however, school is a source of great stress and anxiety. For the unlucky few, it can be hell.

Just because your child is older it does not mean that you no longer have to help him with school work. He may have left spellings and 'reading books' behind, but he needs you now more than ever. It is crucially important to stay involved with your child's school life for a variety of reasons. He spends most of his day at school, so it is important that he is happy there. Exams loom in the teenage years, and these have a knock on effect for college places and future employment prospects. That means it is really important to keep your finger on the pulse of what is going on, so attending any school meetings and open days is very important – they take precedence over work engagements, so factor them in to your diary. Meetings such as this give you the background you need to talk to your teenage child about school. Your interest shows him you care about his future – and that's a vital message to give.

Here's an idea for you...

Encourage your child to develop a small, informal study group with her friends. They can support and motivate each other and homework's more fun (or at least bearable!) when carried out in the company of colleagues. Offer a quiet place in your home for your child and her friends to work, and supply drinks and snacks. Spare pads of paper and a pile of appropriate study guides would also be useful.

EXAM PRESSURE

Firstly, you need to help your child choose the right options to take – which subjects he will study through to examination level. That is very hard, as children are asked to make choices about which path – such as humanities, science or arts – to follow at a young age. Wherever he has a choice about which subjects to take, be led by him. Don't think about what is 'marketable'; instead, think about what he enjoys and what he is good at. It is these subjects that will bring him the greatest success. If he is not interested in the subjects he opts for, it will be a long grind through the years as he works towards taking exams.

When it comes to exam time, give your child as much help as possible – without being invasive. Make sure he has all the resources he needs to revise, such as study guides, notes and appropriate websites. Try to make sure he gets plenty of rest, and takes some nights off too. On the day, encourage him to eat a good but light breakfast, and make sure he has all the equipment he needs ready. If possible, drop him off at school for the exam – it helps to show that you care, and eases any anxiety about missing buses etc.

The school may be putting enormous pressure on him to perform. Schools are increasingly under pressure themselves to do well in league tables – and exam results are an indicator of the school's own success. If your child is academically gifted, he is even more likely to be put under pressure, as the school – and you, and even your child – will have high expectations.

Look out for signs of school stress in your child. If he is moody, listless, depressed and uncommunicative, it may be more than teen attitude – he may be worried about school. Other danger signs include not eating or sleeping properly, apathy and a tendency to avoid contact with school friends.

Are you worried your teenage child may be getting bullied? Check out IDEA 32, _Avoiding ogres and being bullied_, for pointers.

Try another idea…

HELPING WITH HOMEWORK

As a teenager, your child is likely to have a set amount of homework to be completed each night – and this increases as he moves through the school towards exams. It is worth asking about his homework and how it is going – he may not be completing it – going out with friends instead – or it may be overwhelming him.

Your teenager needs a homework routine, with a calm, quiet space and a desk or table for completing work, and supplies such as stationery readily available, as well as access to the family computer.

He may need help with organisation and presentation of his work. If he does not already have a homework timetable from school, help him to create one so that there are no horrible surprises and log jams of work.

'Unhappiness in a child accumulates because he sees no end to the dark tunnel. The thirteen weeks of a term might just as well be thirteen years.'

GRAHAM GREENE

Defining idea…

How did it go?

Q   My teenager has lost interest in school. She was keen when she was younger, but now she has no motivation at all. How can I try to get her interested again?

A   As teens find other things to be interested in – socialising, relationships etc. – school can take the back seat. Without giving a lecture, try to help her understand that to have the things she wants in life, such as a car and a home, she is going to have to work to earn the money to buy them – and the best jobs often go to the people who manage to stick it out at school and get good results. Look for things such as exhibitions and open days that relate to subjects she finds interesting, and go together. If workplaces or colleges are having open days, try to get her to go along for a dose of the inspiration she needs.

Q   I hated school. I did badly and subsequently had to work hard to get qualifications as an adult. My daughter is 13 and seems keen on school so far. How can I keep it that way so she avoids my situation?

A   Try to stay relaxed about school and maintain an interested dialogue with your daughter about what is going on. Offer her encouragement, but don't try to force her to work as a result of your mistakes or you may succeed in turning her off school altogether. Make sure you maintain a dialogue about her work, so you know what she is studying. You can then support her work with visits, relevant books etc.

32

Avoiding ogres and being bullied

Around the world, millions of teenagers are bullied at some time during their school career.

So what do you do if you suspect your teen is being bullied?

Bullying may be characterised by physical or verbal aggression. It is ongoing – and in some cases, unremitting. It is a deliberate attempt to intimidate, threaten or hurt someone. This may be with words and insults, such as teasing or name calling. Teenagers may be bullied by being excluded from a group and their activities, which can be crushing. Your teenager may find herself being criticised constantly about her appearance, schoolwork, or lack of sporting ability. Homophobic bullying is common and highly damaging, as is racist bullying. Such belittling can destroy your child's self-esteem, making it harder for her to withstand the next round of bullying.

Bullying may also be physical, ranging from pushing and jostling to outright violence such as punching and hitting. A campaign of bullying can lead victims to become withdrawn or depressed. Some victims in extreme cases are even driven to suicide.

Here's an idea for you...

If things get really bad, your teenager may need a complete break from school. This is particularly true if the school has been slow to respond to the problem. You may decide to withdraw him from school and educate him at home. School is not compulsory, but education is. You may teach your child at home as long as the education is deemed suitable by the local education authority.
  Check out these helpful websites for more information: 'Education Otherwise' (www.education-otherwise.org/), Homeschool World (http://www.home-school.com/) A–Z Home's Cool (http://homeschooling.gomilpitas.com/).

Your teenager may even be bullied via mobile phone or email. Previously, a bullied teenager may have felt safe once at home, offering some respite. With the advance in technology, teenagers may receive threatening messages by phone message, text or email. This makes them feel exposed even when at home, stripping them of a safe haven, which can be emotionally devastating.

WHO GETS BULLIED?

The stereotypical view of weedy nerds being the butt of teasing and bullying is a comic book cliché. Bullies target a variety of victims, for many different reasons – including just being in the wrong place at the wrong time.

- Kids who look 'different' – they may be tall or small for their age, under or over-weight, dress differently, have different coloured skin
- Kids who act differently to them – they may be very good (or bad) at schoolwork; they may pursue academic rather than sporting hobbies etc.

- Teenagers who are experiencing anxiety or stress – at home or at school.
- Teenagers with special needs or disabilities

What to watch for

Your child *may* be being bullied if:

- Her behaviour changes abruptly, and she seems more withdrawn or moodier than usual, or has problems sleeping.
- She suddenly develops a series of minor illnesses that keep her away from school. She may be avoiding a confrontation. Of course, the threat of bullying and the stress it causes may well bring on symptoms such as stomach and head-aches.
- There are unexplained rips and tears in her clothing, or missing possessions.
- She seems tense or even tearful after school, or talks about hating school and having no friends.

Your teen may be bullied for many reasons – especially if he is 'different' in some way from the mainstream. If he is struggling with peer pressure, check out IDEA 22, *In with the in crowd?*

Try another idea...

TAKE ACTION

Bullying should never be shrugged off, or tolerated. It is a serious problem and your child needs your help to deal with it. Once you have talked the problem through calmly with your child, and reassured her, make a list of the things that have happened to her. Name the

'You've got to fight for your child – if you don't, no one else will.'
MICHELE ELLIOTT of the anti-bullying organisation Kidscape.

Defining idea...

children who are the problem. Then go directly to the school. Take a friend if you need moral support. Schools take bullying seriously, on the whole, and have formulated anti bullying policies to deal with problems.

Calmly state your case to the school representative – your child's class teacher or personal tutor in the first instance. Be assertive and ask the tutor what action will be taken. Your child needs concrete reassurance that bullying will not be tolerated and that she will not suffer from any backlash due to your visit.

If the tutor seems unresponsive or does not take the problem seriously, go straight to the headteacher. Always ask for a follow up appointment to discuss progress on the matter.

COPING STRATEGIES

It is tempting to fly in, all guns blazing when your child is bullied. Before you do your Angelina Jolie impersonation, try to help your child to plan her own strategies for dealing with bullies. This will help to restore her self esteem and will stop her from feeling disempowered.

Some strategies to consider could include:

- staying with a crowd on the way out of school;
- being prepared to yell for help or to run away if necessary;
- building your child's self confidence in things she does well;
- positive imagery – seeing herself ignoring comments in her mind's eye; giving herself the mental blueprint to carry out the plan in real life; and
- imagining an impregnable wall of fire around herself which melts hurtful jibes.

Q   **I have found out from school that my teen is being bullied. I feel awful for not knowing – we talk a lot. How can I make it up to him?**   *How did it go?*

A   *Your child may not have told you through fear – of being seen as a 'grass'; of being a spectacle at school. Don't beat yourself up about it. Tell him you are sorry he has been bearing his ordeal alone, and give him lots of love and reassurance. Take steps to find help for your teen. Counselling may help him to cope with his feelings, and give him strategies to avoid bullying in the future.*

Q   **My son often has abrasions and bruises, and I am worried that he is being bullied. He tells me not to fuss. What can I do?**

A   *The marks may just be the result of ordinary horseplay, or your son may just be temporarily clumsy, but they may be indicators of a problem. Without making a big deal of it, perhaps offer him some arnica cream and ask how the marks occurred. Do not let the matter drop. Your son may be afraid to tell you what is going on for fear of making things worse.*

33

'What did your last maid die of?'

We are all busy – most of us working out of the house every day. Household chores are squashed into tired after-work sessions, or eat into what should be a restful weekend.

Add a teenager or two to the mix, and the house can descend into chaos. If this sounds like your house, you need a plan!

If you think your house is too far gone, and you are planning to wait until your teenagers have moved out to disinfect the house and redecorate – think again! You can salvage things and reclaim your house.

As you look around and see your untidy house in all its glory, remember one thing. Apart from a couple of close friends, you probably don't often see other people's houses in their natural state. You assume everyone else is tidier than you, and keeps a cleaner house because that is what they choose you to see. Can you honestly say that you don't run round cleaning up when you know visitors are on their way? I have been known to hide things away in weird places – ovens, dishwashers, crammed into the video unit … Other people get that impression from your house too, and the cycle of feeling inadequate continues.

Put a basket or plastic box for each family member in the cupboard under the stairs or any other hidden but accessible place. When you find 'stuff' cluttering rooms, dump it in the appropriate box. Then pick a time, perhaps at the weekend, when boxes are expected to be emptied and things put away. If you are tight for space, use one big glory box and people can rummage for their stuff – if they don't like it, they should put their stuff away. Be prepared to take a hard line if your teenager doesn't empty the box as instructed; tell her it goes in a bin bag if it is not put away by the deadline, because she obviously does not value the item.

Before you tackle your untidy teenager, check out how your own clean and tidy routine runs. Is it carried out as a quick 'binge' when you can't find floor space to walk? I've tried it, and it actually gets depressing after a while. I don't need my house to be *uber* tidy, but I can't work looking at a pile of dishes and with clutter from one end of the house to another. Think about your own comfort threshold, rather than thinking what your house *should* look like. This is different for everybody, but it gives you a 'bottom line' of how you want your house to look – and that's a good starting point.

Once you have found your comfort threshold, break the news to your family that there is going to be a new way of doing things. Explain that when the house is really grotty, it gets you down (and ignore the sighs and eye rolling that may accompany this news). Tell your teens (and younger children) that you think it would be fair if they all tidy up after themselves in communal areas such as the bathroom, kitchen and living room. Point out that if this was done there would be a lot less nagging to listen to as you would no longer feel resentful as you picked up dirty wet towels, dishes etc. Work out rules together that your teens can accept, which satisfy your comfort threshold.

Is your teen's room a mess too? Check out IDEA 34, *Wallowing in the sty – your teenager's room***, for tips on the way out of the tip!**

Try another idea…

You have to back up this suggested change of routine with details. Teenagers often need very precise instructions. In our house, for example, we had to mention that 'doing the dishes' did not just mean filling the dishwasher; it also meant hand washing anything too delicate or that did not fit in the washer. Clearly state your expectations for tasks. For example, if your teenager makes a snack, he should tidy up after himself, putting packets, jars etc. back in cupboards and wiping surfaces etc.

Use deadlines when you ask your teenager to do a job. Again, be specific. Instead of saying, 'Please tidy away your clothes and toiletries from the bathroom', say 'Please tidy away your clothes and toiletries from the bathroom before supper.' This means he has a window to carry out tasks and are less likely to rebel than if you say 'do it now' and keep nagging until it is done; it also avoids the problem of the job never quite getting done because he doesn't get round to it.

Apart from shared areas, your teenager should expect to have a specific task or chore. In our house, our kids take turns to do the dishes

'They never put on a woman's gravestone "She kept a tidy house".'
MARGARET McSEVENEY, playwright

Defining idea…

after dinner, and tend to the animals and pets. I know other families where they empty the bins, vacuum the shared rooms, sweep the patio etc. This helps to spread household chores and gives a vital message about communal living and responsibility – to boys and girls.

Q **I love all these plans – but what if my daugher doesn't comply?**

How did it go?

A *You need sanctions to back up your new system. Make it clear that there are consequences if jobs are not done. Tailor these to your daughter. The prospect of no pocket money is a good incentive for most teens. Alternatively, refuse to do jobs for her whilst she is being unhelpful. Say you will not give lifts etc. until she complies, as you are spending extra time doing jobs she should be doing, so you have no spare time to ferry her around.*

Q **My son often seems to have a huge stash of dishes in his room which periodically emerge green with mould, to be left in the kitchen. What can I do?**

A *Send him on 'dish missions' each evening before the dishwasher is put on or the dishes are done. If he still leaves dishes in his room, dock his pocket money until he complies.*

34

Wallowing in the sty: your teenager's room

Does your teenager's room drive you mad? Is it a grungy mess with very little floor space?

Should you help clean it up, or is that invading her space? Should you even care about the state of her room?

Many parents moan about the state of their teenagers' rooms. I am a fairly untidy person myself and have a high mess threshold – so I am not too phased about my teens' rooms. As long as the door still shuts, there are no pongs or vermin (dodgy friends do not count!), and they don't take my stuff into their rooms I'm not too bothered. If you are the same, congratulations – it makes life less stressful. If you are bothered, however, there are things you can do to make things better.

Sometimes, teenagers' rooms can give the impression that there has been an explosion in a clothing factory, with CDs and other teenage ephemera liberally thrown into the mix, including strange green fuzzy mugs that may or may not contain a vital science experiment (or new, previously undiscovered form of life).

Here's an idea for you…

If your teenager is at a loss because his room is so heinous, go in with him and help. Take three black bin bags: one for rubbish, one for stuff that needs a home and one for the charity shop. Some kids find it easier to give things away if they know it is going to make someone else happy, and a charity shop does this twice. This activity has the added bonus of getting across the value of 'reuse' as apposed to throwing things away; it can also embed the idea of giving to a charitable cause. You can also offer goods on freecycle (find a local group at www. freecycle.org).
Some people keep this third box of goods to sell at a car boot or yard sale. Their children are allowed to keep the money made on their own goods – quite an incentive!

Teenagers are usually, by their very nature, secretive – even if they have nothing much to hide! Try to treat your teenager's room as private space. It goes without saying that you should not rummage about in her room – how invaded would you feel if she carried out a search of your private possessions? Respect her space, but set boundaries too, according to what makes you comfortable. It may be no smoking (including guests), or all food to be cleared away daily including dishes etc.

GIVE HER A HEAD START

Being organised isn't always easy. It is a learned skill. When you tell your teenager to tidy her room, she may look at you blankly – not necessarily because it's an alien concept but because she is not sure how to tackle the momentous task ahead. Some teens, asked to tidy up, push everything together into a pile on the bed – and then they are not sure what to do with it. So it gets crammed into drawers, piled in the wardrobe and shoved under the bed. Everything looks tidy – until they need something and pull everything out again.

Help your teenager to develop a routine. She should make her bed, open a window, put away homework papers/books/stationery, and pile her dirty clothes in the washing basket. She should put rubbish in the bin – and newsflash this, to many teens – empty the bin weekly. Any towels should be folded for reuse or put in the laundry bin if they need washing.

If your teen's tidal wave of junk is threatening to envelop the house, read IDEA 33, '*What did your last maid die of?*', for coping strategies.

Try another idea…

Make sure your teenager has easy storage for her stuff – shelves for books and CDs, storage boxes for other bits and pieces. She can't put it away if there is nowhere for it to go!

HELP TO CREATE A SANCTUARY

Once she shows an interest (even the tiniest stirring) in keeping her room tidy, offer her a chance to have a room makeover. It needn't be expensive. Changing her room from the frilly palace she wanted to create at the age of 12 to a cooler, more adult space may be all the encouragement she needs.

Set a budget according to your means, and encourage your teenager to choose her own paint and accessories. If she feels more ownership of her room, she is more likely to keep it tidy. Make sure you provide plenty of storage such as under-the-bed boxes. A book-shelf equipped with cheap square baskets looks attractive and hides a multitude of sins, as well as separating different small items such

'If your house is really a mess and a stranger comes to the door, greet him with, "Who could have done this? We have no enemies!"'
PHYLLIS DILLER,
American comedienne and actress,
(born 1917)

Defining idea…

151

as cosmetics, computer games etc. so they are easier to find. A desk with shelves above will help her to keep her schoolbooks and assignments from getting lost. Give her a laundry hamper for dirty clothes, which she can bring down to the washing machine herself. Add candles, posters, rugs etc. that she has chosen, and she gets a sanctuary – and you hopefully get one less source of conflict.

How did it go?

Q   My son drops clean clothes in a pile on the floor where they mingle with dirty clothes. I end up washing heaps more than I need to. What can I do?

A   *Give your son two baskets, one for clean clothes and one for dirty. Tell him he needs to take dirty clothes downstairs to the utility room. If he doesn't comply, tell him he has to be responsible for his own washing.*

Q   I never mean to, but I often end up tidying up for my son – I just can't bear his room to look so bad. It's getting me down – what can I do?

A   *Your son needs see the consequences of his behaviour. Teach him what to do, then leave him to it. If he can't find his shirt for a hot date because it's in a pile of stuff on the floor – tough luck. It sounds hard, but if you are always there to make things right, he will never learn. A little inconvenience will teach him a valuable lesson.*

35

24-hour party people

The words 'teenage parties' fill many parents with dread.

But by agreeing some basic rules and using simple coping strategies, hosting teenage parties can be problem free — and even fun!

There is no need to be scared of teenage parties. Despite the wild debauchery seen in films such as the *American Pie* series, the average teenage party is a much more sedate affair. As our house is in the middle of a field, we have often hosted teenage parties, as the noise doesn't disturb the neighbours (unless you count the goats). They have ranged from small, organised Halloween parties for young teenagers to large, noisy parties for older teenagers – and we have enjoyed them all despite the effort involved.

By taking a few precautions, you can enjoy your teenager's parties too. It is important to welcome your teenager's friends and your child will appreciate being able to play host, especially at parties to mark events such as special birthdays and exam success.

Here's an idea for you... **Make sure your teen does not just offer an open invitation via SMS and texts to 'whoever' – you need to know that only the number your house can cope with will turn up. She should physically make an agreed number of invitations on the PC and hand them out. When deciding on numbers, consider the space available including kitchen and bathroom facilities.**

You can decide to hold a party at an outside venue, which removes many of the worries you may have about property damage etc. – but of course there is a cost involved. If you host a party at home, there are things you can do to make things run smoothly.

SHOULD I STAY OR SHOULD I GO?

If you have young teenagers, do not even consider leaving the party. You will be needed to make sure things run smoothly and do not get out of hand. For older teens, you could consider leaving for a while or go to another part of the house. Personally, I prefer to remain at the party and enjoy the company on the whole. My teens have never objected to my presence – I do keep filling up the dishes and getting clean glasses after all! However, if you do stay, do not try to join in the fun unless invited – teens are easily embarrassed when dad shows off his moves on the dance floor or mum gets giggly and flirtatious.

Some teenagers (like some adults) are careless of other people's property. It is sensible to pack away delicate valuables and ornaments before the party – I even do this before adult parties. It is not being suspicious or untrusting to lock away precious items – it just removes worries.

Agree to any rules you may wish to enforce ahead of the party. During a party is not a time to argue with your teenager about arrangements. Don't be heavy handed, but talk about the rules you need in order to feel comfortable about hosting a party. Rules might include no smoking in the house, and some rooms in your house (such as your bedroom, for example) being off-limits. Identify a secure room where bags and coats can be kept. Make it clear to your teen that you expect him to help prepare for and clean up after the party; it is fun to invite a few guests to help with preparations and having a few extra pairs of hands after the party is also useful.

If your teen is breaking curfew, read IDEA 17, *What time do you call this?*, for tips on reinstating the rules.

Try another idea…

Alcohol is a potentially thorny issue. Do not provide alcohol for young teenagers and make it clear that guests are not to bring any. Some may, of course, be smuggled in, but all you can do is try your best. Offer a variety of no alcohol beers or punch, and plenty of soft drinks. Beer shandy is very popular with young teens – especially boys! Be careful to watch any punch you make so that nobody spikes it – having a spare adult to act as 'barman' gets around this problem.

With older teenagers, supply beer and perhaps wine at an 18th birthday party. Supply plenty of soft drinks. Do not forget that some older teens prefer not to drink, and some may be designated drivers. Keep an eye on things to make sure nobody is making themselves ill by drinking too much – it's not good for those involved and can be bad for your soft furnishings! Once again, a 'barman' can be a good idea to slow the flow of alcohol. Offer food too to help to counter

'I am thankful for the mess to clean after a party because it means I have been surrounded by friends.'
NANCIE J. CARMODY

Defining idea…

the effects of alcohol. It is worth locking away or moving your own alcohol or you may be horrified to discover your oak aged malt has disappeared …

If any of those present seem very drunk, perhaps vomiting, consider phoning their parents to come and pick them up. If parents are unavailable – or unwilling (it happens!) – have contingency plans. This may involve keeping the young guest in a quiet room and keeping an eye on him. Excessive alcohol consumption by teenagers who are young or inexperienced can be very dangerous and can require medical intervention.

How did it go?

Q   Should I warn my neighbours my daughter is having a party?

A   *Yes – if they are forewarned, they may decide to go out for the evening. Explain to your daughter that music will have to be turned down after a certain agreed time. Set a finishing time for the party, and supervise the departure of guests to avoid a noisy congregation of young people in the street. If you find out early in the evening if guests need taxis, you can book them early.*

Q   What happens if there are gatecrashers?

A   *Politely ask uninvited guests to leave. I have done this on several occasions and have been firm and confident but non aggressive and there has not been a problem. (I'm only 5'2" – so I don't think it was because I looked imposing or scary). Unlikely though it is to be necessary, if at any point you feel things are out of control, threaten to call the police, and then do so if you have to.*

36

And in the blue corner ...

Are you sick of the teasing and fighting that goes on in your house? Can the personalities clashing be heard on distant continents?

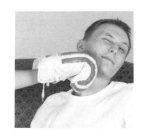

There are ways to beat the bickering.

Some friction is natural between siblings – try to take it as a given, rather than a reflection on the harmony in your home! Arguing over anything – or even everything – is quite normal at this stage of development. If you have brothers and sisters yourself, you will probably be able to remember some fairly spectacular arguments from your own teen years. Conflict is a fact of life, and the family is a safe place to learn all about life skills such as negotiation and problem solving. Learning how to deal with negative emotions will help your teen to mature, and build relationships outside of the family.

Be vigilant, however, that play fighting and teasing does not deteriorate into thinly disguised bullying.

However, although no one is likely to get hurt by routine spats, you may start to feel worn down by the constant background squabbling. That goes on in the healthiest of families. So what can you do?

Here's an idea for you...

Try to de-escalate arguments by diverting your teenage children. Give them a job to do, or send one on an errand to break the tension. You should also encourage them to solve their own problems and differences. If you wade in, you disempower them and put them back into 'child' mode. Although intervention is sometimes necessary, develop a facilitator role. Sit down as a family and talk things through, taking the heat out of the situation. Paraphrasing views with non emotive language is a great start, and your children will learn by your example.

IDENTIFY THE TRIGGERS

Tiredness

Do your teens fight more in the evening, after a long day at school? They may be tired and thus more volatile and prone to squabbling. Plan relaxing evening activities such as watching a film together or reading and listening to music, and see if this helps to calm the atmosphere.

Possessions

If there are regular fights about particular things, encourage your teens to establish rules about sharing – particular times of the day, or days of the week for example. If they devise the rules themselves, they are more likely to keep them.

Space

Sibling arguments are often, essentially, about space. If they share a room, let them divide it in an agreed way. My sister and I shared a room as teenagers and the demarcation was created by walls full of posters – Osmonds on my side of the room; David Cassidy on hers …

It may also be worth thinking about putting locks on their bedroom doors if 'space invasion' – by siblings, rather than little green men – is a problem. If a sibling does not respect space, and goes into her brother's bedroom to borrow things or just nose around, she needs to be told firmly that this is unacceptable. Everyone in the family needs an inviolate space where they can have privacy from the demands of family life.

If your son creates a war zone wherever he goes, check out IDEA 9, *Fight club: how to avoid arguments, and de-escalation tactics*, for creating some calm.

Try another idea...

Jockeying for position

Your teens may argue as they try to create their own position within the family hierarchy. It may be that your eldest child feels threatened by a younger sibling who is 'catching up' with her in abilities, academically etc. and is threatening her perceived 'primacy.' Make sure that you do not overestimate the maturity of your eldest child, expecting too much from her just because she is the eldest and 'should know better'.

If your teens are being excessively competitive, watch out for comments and behaviour that belittle the sibling's achievements. Give lots of positive reinforcement to both of them, and make sure you do not make comparisons between them. They are all different, and have different skills and aptitudes. Celebrate these without comparing. Help insecure teens to find and develop their strengths and thus their confidence. Let them know you value their particular abilities.

'Discussion is an exchange of knowledge; an argument an exchange of ignorance.'
ROBERT QUILLEN

Defining idea...

How did it go?

Q **My teenage childrens fight all the time – they just seem to rub each other up the wrong way. What can I do?**

A *Sometimes within families there are personality clashes that make it diffi-cult for people to get along together. This can be particularly true of teens and adolescents, who may be more volatile than the rest of the family, and flare ups can occur with monotonous regularity. Sit them down and tell them that you know they are having lots of arguments and this is disturb-ing for the rest of the family. Ask them to work out compromises between themselves when they have an argument. They will find this difficult, and you may have to act as referee to begin with, but it is worth persevering.*

Q **My son constantly says that I side with his sister, who is appar-ently my 'favourite'. How can I reassure him that this is not the case?**

A *Be brutally honest with yourself and first make sure there is no favourit-ism in your home. A teen who feels that a parent is constantly siding with a sibling will feel raging jealousy – even if the slights are imagined. Make sure you do not spend more time with one teen than another. If there is any bias in your behaviour, change it immediately. If the bias is perceived but you honestly do not feel that it is justified, think about why your son feels this way. He may just be feeling the need for a little extra time and attention at the moment – so be ready to spend time with her to make her feel more secure.*

37

No *means* no!

**Children need consistency from birth – and the need is
just as strong for teenagers.**

*Consistency minimises arguments and
helps your child to develop a sense of
responsibility — so read on to find out how
it may be achieved!*

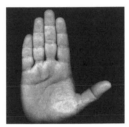

From the day your child is born, he learns by processing the messages that he
receives – emotional, instructional, and educational. In order for him to make sense
of those messages, he needs them to be consistent. Knowing his routine and the
reactions he can expect from you has helped him to become a secure and balanced
person. The need for consistency does not disappear once your child grows into his
teenage years; if anything, he needs it now more than ever as he tests his – and your
– boundaries, and grows up into a responsible adult.

Inconsistency can be confusing for teenagers because of the message it gives them.
Think about it: your 14-year-old daughter attends a family party and is encouraged
by well meaning but ill informed family members to have several drinks. She gets

Here's an idea for you... **Make sure you and your partner are consistent when it comes to parenting. Come to an agreement between you in private. Make an effort to discuss matters between the pair of you before you speak to your teenager so that there is some semblance of agreement. If you need time to discuss an issue before coming to a decision, tell your teen you need a little time and will get back to her shortly. In that way, your teen (however sweet) will not be able to play you off, one against the other.**
If one parent is laissez faire and the other is disciplinarian, you are in for a bumpy ride! You are different people with different temperaments; you had different upbringings and your views on behaviour are not going to be seamlessly joined, even if they are similar.

a little drunk and starts to act in a silly way. Family members think it is funny, and act indulgently – after all, they know she is in a safe environment with her family. You smile ruefully, chuckle and cart her off home to bed to sleep it off at the end of the evening. Your teen has had fun and no harm is done. Or is it? A message was unwittingly given to your daughter. It said that drinking too much alcohol is amusing and fun, and older members of the family – including you – think it is OK.

Now, fast forward a month or so. Your daughter has been to a 16th birthday party, unsupervised by adults. She has been given plenty of alcohol to drink, and is well on the way to being drunk. As you pull into the car park at the venue to pick her up at a pre-arranged time, she is wrapped round an older boy you do not recognise in a hot and heavy embrace. You are shocked, and call her sharply. She traipses back to the car eventually and is sick on the back seat on the way home. You are furious. Apart from having to use the swab-and-bicarb routine on the car upholstery, you have nightmare flashes of what might have happened to her if you had not arrived at that opportune moment. You react the next day with ranting and raving, and ground her for a month.

Now – think for a minute. You seemed to condone her drinking in the first example, but condemn it in the second. Your teen is confused because of your inconsistency. You can see the difference – in the first example, she was under your beady eye and had the backup of her whole family to keep her safe. In the second situation, she was to all intents and purposes on her own, with no safety net.

Make sure you are 'walking the walk' before you 'talk the talk' and avoid arguments. Read IDEA 40, *Don't do as I do...*, to find out more.

Try another idea...

All your teenager sees though is the confusing way in which you are behaving. She feels angry and resentful towards you, because she had received the message that drinking to excess was OK, and even amusing – and then suddenly she is in trouble for the same behaviour. Instead of learning about acceptable and sensible behaviour, she has learned that you are unfair and irrational – which, of course, she always suspected. Inconsistency leads to arguments – if not all out rebellion. Your teen is more likely to test boundaries when the boundaries are firmly set. That does not mean no flexibility is allowed; it means rather that your teenager knows that 'no' means 'no' in the same way as she did when she was a child. Consistency from you will teach your teen that actions lead to consequences – and that is good for her future decision making skills.

'Consistency is the last refuge of the unimaginative.'

OSCAR WILDE, Irish dramatist, novelist and poet (1854–1900)

Defining idea...

How did it go?

Q **I find it really hard to be consistent with my son, especially when I am tired. Is it really so important?**

A *It is hard to be consistent, especially when you are tired and want an easy ride. Not imposing sanctions for a missed curfew isn't the end of the world, but if you give him too many chances to break rules and get away without consequences, you are encouraging him to push those boundaries even further. Do yourself a favour and maintain consistency to reduce arguments in the future.*

Q **We seem to have different standards of behaviour to our son's school, which is rather strict, and this is causing difficulties. We want to support the school and maintain consistency discipline-wise, but let our son know that our standards are different. Will this cause difficulties?**

A *One of the lessons teenagers need to learn is how to cope with differences between the outside world and the family in terms of values and mores. Your son needs to learn how to deal with, and react appropriately to, different situations and sets of rules. Handled sensitively, this difference can be used to help this process of adjustment. Talk to your son and explain that your standards are different to those of his school. Discuss the differences, and any problems this may potentially cause. It may be that you find the divide between your views and those of the school too wide. If this is the case, you may need to consider a different school.*

38

You can't make me!

We should expect our teens to rebel; it is part of becoming an adult, and showing they have their own minds.

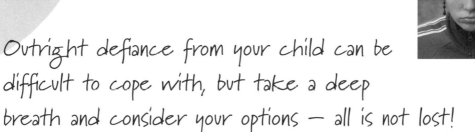

Outright defiance from your child can be difficult to cope with, but take a deep breath and consider your options — all is not lost!

'Teenage' and 'rebellion' – the words flow naturally together. It's almost a cliché. We rebelled against our parents; in turn our own teenagers rebel against us and our cherished ideals. It is a fact of life that teenagers row with their parents. They are testing the water; finding the limits of their power and influence.

Your teenager daughter may be defiant for a variety of reasons. It may be that she is feeling stifled and over protected; she may feel she is being treated unfairly (don't all teenagers feel this?). She may defy your wishes simply because she does not agree with them or she may be in a state of permanent defiance because she is used to getting her own way.

Here's an idea for you...

If your teenager is defiant and rude to you, take a deep breath and calmly explain to him that you would not accept this behaviour from another adult. Tell him that if he insists on talking to you in this way you will not listen – you would ignore a persistently abusive adult. Then move to another room. It may initially make him angry, but he needs to learn the lesson that this behaviour is unacceptable, even in adults. If you shout and yell back, you are validating his behaviour with attention. Stop it dead in its tracks and be prepared to persist with this strategy; it is hard to do, but it works.

Her rebellion may even be symbolic. She wants to impress her peers and find her place in the world. If you disapprove of her behaviour, all the better. She may be defying you as a way of asserting her independence and 'grown up' status.

Some researchers even see rows as a positive event – but perhaps they are not parents of teenagers, feeling bruised and battered from the latest round of conflict! Some behavioural scientists believe that when teenagers argue with their parents, they are actually learning how to negotiate – a vital life skill. Your teenage child is pushing boundaries and practicing negotiation skills in a safe environment.

The fact is that your teenager needs to break away from you and your influence if she is to become an adult on her own terms. Whilst it is true that she needs to take charge of her own life, that does not mean there is not still a place for you, your influence and ideals. You have a whole life ahead of you where you are parent to your adult child, and it can be a fabulous experience. You are working towards a peer relationship with your own child as she becomes an adult. The problem is, neither of you knows how to act as equals; as the parent, you have been used to being in the position of power. You have to learn to give that up now. The key to managing defiance and rebellion in your teenager is to treat her increasingly as an adult whilst protecting her at the same time. As she gets older, you remove more of the 'parental safety net' to allow her to become an adult standing on her own two feet (but still with you there as an in-the-shadows back up). Riding out the rough moments as the transition is made can be hard, but hang in there for the long haul and it will be worth it.

If you feel that you can't talk with your teen without arguing, read IDEA 9, *Fight club: how to avoid arguments, and de-escalation tactics*, for tips on staying calm and reducing arguments.

Try another idea...

MAKE SOME BREATHING SPACE

When you are feeling embattled by your teenager's seemingly constant rebellion – which can seem at times to be done just for the sake of getting a rise out of you – step back and make breathing space for yourself. It is easy to fall in to a pattern of antagonism where you expect rebellion, defiance and rudeness at every turn – and that then can become a self-fulfilling prophecy. You expect your child to be defiant and your attitude shows it; the cycle persists.

'Here are three ways to get something done: do it yourself, employ someone, or forbid your children to do it.'
MONTA CRANE

Defining idea...

How did it go?

Q   I feel as though my son and I are locked in permanent battle – how can I break out of the loop?

A   *Pick your battles. Be prepared to let small things go and your son will have less to rebel against. Remember that your parenting goal is to encourage him to live his own life, with his own set of values.*

Q   Sometimes, although it sounds awful, I find it quite hard to really like my son – I get so tired of all the battles. Is this normal?

A   *Very much so – don't beat yourself up! Look at photos of your child growing up. He is the same person inside, albeit overlaid with more attitude. Think about how much you love him, however difficult your relationship can be at times. These difficulties will pass.*

Try to remember that your son will sometimes wonder why your relationship can be so stormy too. He may feel at a loss as to how to break the cycle of anger and resentment that can arise. Don't be afraid to reach through the barrier sometimes. Remember to praise him when he is helpful; remember to maintain some sort of loving physical contact with him. You may be a 'touchy-feely' family that enjoys hugs – if so, great. But if not, try just squeezing his arm or shoulder affectionately sometimes in passing. Teenagers may be quite lonely for affection in a sometimes difficult transitional period between childhood and being an adult. They may feel too big to be openly affectionate with you, but may not have a partner to be affectionate with. Basically, we all need human contact, even if it just consists of a rough and tumble play fight between a teenager and his dad.

39

Take it back! Saying things you regret

They may say 'Sticks and stones make break my bones; words will never hurt me' – but they are wrong.

Words can wound. Sometimes the echoes of words said years before follow us through our lives, affecting our decisions and choices.

As the parent of teenage children, you can be stretched to your limit. There is no such thing as a perfect parent, and when you are tired or angry you can sometimes say something you regret immediately – or even later when the scene drifts back into your head.

Imagine this scene: your fifteen-year-old daughter is getting ready to go out. She comes downstairs dressed in a skimpy T-shirt and skirt combo. She thinks she looks great; you tell her to go upstairs and change; she refuses. An argument ensues. You end up telling her she dresses like a tart, and she slams off upstairs in floods of tears. All you wanted to do was keep her safe …

Here's an idea for you...

If you say something really hurtful, don't be afraid to apologise to your teenager. (and the same goes for younger children, or other adults). Tell your teen you are sorry, and you should never have said the hurtful comment. Tell her you know it was unkind and you don't mean it. Don't try to make excuses (none are valid after all) but do let her know any reasons for your outburst. It may be that you are tired, or that you have had a rough day at work. It doesn't make things OK, but it does allow your teenager to contextualise your behaviour. Letting her know the reasons for your own 'bad behaviour' will also make her feel more adult and trusted by you as a confidant. Finally, offer a hug and try to make up. If she rejects your apology, try not to take it personally – the effort you have made will have registered and will pay dividends.

Scene two: your seventeen-year-old son seems to be slacking off at school. He's going out every night and you are worried that he is ruining his chances for a place at college. He tells you he is doing enough work to get by and you should keep out of his business. You flare up and tell him he is lazy and will end up working in a dead end job. He slams the door on his way out. All you wanted to do was to make sure he made the most of his chances …

Similar scenes are carried out in homes around the world. They don't make you a bad parent; you have your child's welfare at heart. However, the name calling and negative self image you are projecting onto your child can have repercussions. If a teenager is subjected to a barrage of criticism and negative comments it will wear him down. If your child hears this type of comment regularly, he may internalise the feelings and images, and this can be destructive.

Try to think before you speak rather than letting words tumble out of your mouth. It's hard, and you will make mistakes (you are only human) but it is worth the effort.

WHAT YOU SAY CREATES BLUEPRINTS

Be careful about the roles you unwittingly assign your children. If you constantly refer to one child as the academically gifted child, or another as the artistic or sporty child, you can set a blueprint for the self image your child carries in his head. Not so bad if he is the academic one (although it puts him under pressure to succeed) but if he is the child seen even jokingly as 'the clumsy one' or the 'more practical (read "dumb") one' it can be rather crushing.

As if there was not enough pressure upon you already, the things you say about yourself can also erode your teen's self confidence. If you routinely overreact in a theatrical fashion to situations, talking in absolutes such as: 'I just can't take the pressure at work' or 'I never have any luck', your teen may find it hard to develop an optimistic outlook on life. Verbalise your problems by all means – but then talk about ways you are considering to handle those problems. If you can't handle the pressure at work, perhaps you need to talk to a superior, or even think about changing roles. This will help your teen to develop an 'I can' attitude rather than a pessimistic beaten one. It's better for you too!

Finding it hard to communicate with your teenager? Check out IDEA 14, *Making time*, for some ideas.

Try another idea…

'The words that a father speaks to his children in the privacy of home are not heard by the world, but, as in whispering galleries, they are clearly heard at the end, and by posterity.'

JEAN PAUL RICHTER, novelist

Defining idea…

How did
it go?

Q My parents were very critical of me, ridiculing things I did and often using sarcasm that hurt me. It has taken me a long time to develop a positive self image. Do you have any tips on how to be positive with my own teens?

A *You are a step ahead of many parents as you are aware of the damage that can be done, sometimes unwittingly. How about telling your teens how wonderful they are? Praise them regularly, and let them know what great people they are. This will help them to feel good about themselves and will help them to develop a positive outlook on life. Don't forget the plentiful hugs and affection!*

Q I try hard but often seem to fly off the handle and say things I regret later. How can I avoid this?

A *If you are arguing with your teen and you feel yourself reaching boiling point, give yourself some 'time out'. You might say 'I am very angry. I need to go away and think about how to deal with this situation and I'll come talk with you in a few minutes.' Leave the room; have a cup of tea. When you have calmed down, go back to her and talk about the problem. Make sure you are taking enough time out for yourself. Read a book, have a massage, go for reiki – bring down your stress levels and you will be more likely to cope.*

40

Don't do as I do ...

Do you remember the old adage 'Don't do as I do, do as I tell you'? It doesn't work where teens are concerned.

Teens can smell hypocrisy a mile off — and they listen much more closely to what you do than what you say.

We all probably want our children to grow up to be strong characters, capable of facing difficult challenges, who persevere even when things get tough. This development begins when they are very small, and it is shaped by their life experiences. They are praised and rewarded for doing well and acting kindly and told off and have to face consequences for their actions. These things help them develop into the adults they will one day become.

Very young children learn by mimicking the behaviour of the adults who care for them. You taught your children to wash their hands by showing them how. You taught them how to tie their shoe laces by copying you. You showed them how to do these things by following your own example. You showed your child many things as she grew older, and not all of them deliberately. You shaped your teenager's development by the way you act and speak, and live your life.

Here's an idea for you...

Preach what you practice. Model the behaviour you want your teenager to adopt. This is more effective if you talk about what you are doing and why. If you work as a volunteer on a community project, for example, your children are more likely to copy your behaviour and volunteer for things themselves if you share your motivation. Tell them the reasons why you are working as a volunteer, such as to make your community a better place; you have skills to offer that others may not have etc.

Your teen will not be fooled by a smokescreen. There is no point telling her to act in one way, but acting in another way yourself. The way you act with family, friends, work colleagues and the wider world speaks volumes. You cannot just talk about ideals with your teens; you have to live by them daily, modelling caring, loving and responsible behaviour so they can see its importance. Having a child is like having a bright light shone into your soul, exposing your deepest held values. Having a teenager is like having the same torch – with a cynical commentator attached.

MONKEY SEE, MONKEY DO

Think about it – if you tell your teenage daughter not to drink too much when she goes out with her friends, but she regularly sees you drinking heavily, why should she listen? If you tell her not to drink and drive, but slide behind the wheel after 'just a couple' at a barbecue – how will you convince her that drinking and driving is dangerous? After all, you do it and nothing bad ever happens. Do you expect your teens to treat you with respect? Do you consistently show that you value your partner and children? Do you treat your own parents, wider family, friends, and colleagues with respect? If not, why should your teen listen to your advice? Do you tell your teen to 'watch her language' but spend car journeys swearing and cursing at other drivers? Why should she listen to you?

If you tell your daughter to work hard at school, but regularly cut corners at work, just doing what you need to get by, why should she? If you tell your teenage son to be respectful to women, but then have a stack of girlie mags, what is going to shout louder? Your behaviour or your hollow words? Do you expect your teenagers to show self-discipline and to be able to control their temper enough to discuss disputes rather than have a shouting match? What are you doing to set an example? Do you cope calmly with crises, or do you meet problems and disagreements with anger and rage? Your teenager will see through you, and will not listen. Youth hates hypocrisy with a passion, above most other things.

Nobody is saying that you have to be perfect to be a parent – and nobody can be perfect. It is not always easy to do the right thing, or to stand up for your beliefs, or to speak out when you think someone has been treated unfairly. There are times when we all fall short because we are feeling too tired to make the effort, or we are worried about repercussions. But if you generally act in a way that you would be happy for your teenagers to observe – or copy – you are helping to develop a new adult to be proud of.

Are you having trouble with consistency? Read IDEA 37, *No* means *no!*, for some pointers.

Try another idea...

'*The only way to raise a decent human being is by being one.*'
EDA LESHAN, a family counsellor and author

Defining idea...

How did it go?

Q **I want to teach my teenage son to be frugal and save, but I have in the past run up lots of consumer debt. Can I teach him to learn from my mistakes?**

A *You can certainly warn him about how easy it is for people's debts to escalate. Warn him, but then teach him by your present example – let him know that you put money away each month, and show him the other things you do to save money, such as buying vintage instead of new, buying in bulk, sharing rides to work.*

Q **Can I teach my teens ethics by pointing out the consequences of the behaviour of other people?**

A *Well, it may be better to avoid pointing the finger at friends and neighbours! Instead, take advantage of things in everyday life or in the news and talk about them to reinforce the ethics you hope your teens will adopt. Don't preach, but ask questions – or they will tune you out. Rather than avoiding or ignoring the latest scandal on the news, talk about it. Ask your teenagers what they think about what has happened, and the consequences of the scandal for those involved.*

You can also point out people in your community who are showing positive behaviour such as supporting their family, rising to the challenge that illness and unemployment can bring etc. Accentuate the positive!

41

Coping with the 'tin grin': living with a brace

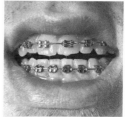

Everyone from Tom Cruise to Gwen Stefani has been wearing braces recently in the pursuit of a glitteringly smooth smile.

But what do you do if an appointment with the orthodontist has left your teenage child feeling down in the mouth?

Your teenager may need braces to correct crooked teeth, or if he has an underbite (where the bottom jaw is bigger) or an overbite (where the top jaw bone is bigger). Whatever the reason, he's unlikely to come dancing out of the orthodontists when he hears that he needs a brace.

The most common type of brace is made up of small brackets that are put on the surface of the teeth and strung together with a strip of wire. Braces put pressure on the teeth to help them to move into the correct position in the mouth.

Here's an idea for you…

Be sensitive about timing where getting a brace is concerned. It may be inevitable that your teenager needs a brace if she wants straight teeth, but where there is flexibility she should be involved in making the decision about timing. There may be a special occasion in the near future, such as a big birthday party, where she may be worried about photos. She may prefer to think about having her braces fitted before the long summer break so she can get used to wearing them before facing the crowds at school. The important thing is to listen to her concerns and try to accommodate her wishes. Discuss any issues with your orthodontist, and make a joint decision. This is something that is happening to your child and she will feel much more empowered and in control if she has some say in the matter.

Braces are usually metal, but you can get also get plastic brackets that are either clear, for invisibility, or even brightly coloured to match your child's personality!

Firstly, the orthodontist will make a mould of the teeth with resin. X rays will also be taken to help to make any decisions about any extractions that need to be made. It is quite common for this to be necessary when there is overcrowding. I can tell you from bitter experience that having looked after your child's teeth from the word go, encouraging brushing twice daily, arranging visits from the tooth fairy and limiting sugary snacks it is appalling to have to stand by and watch strong, healthy teeth being extracted – but sometimes it is necessary. My eldest son had extractions and a brace for two years – and now has an amazing smile – and he says it was all worth it.

After the 'trackline' is attached to the teeth, rubber bands or elastics are attached to hold the brace in place. They are a vital part of the process, exerting pressure to move the teeth in directions that braces alone cannot. These elastics need changing daily, and not wearing them can make the treatment slow or even useless. At first, your teen may find applying the elastics tricky, but he will become adept after a while – probably after some hilarity and elastics pinging off walls, the dog etc.

Boost your teen's self esteem with praise – read IDEA 30, *Positive parenting: the power of praise*, for ways to give her a boost.

Try another idea...

For a few days after your teen has a brace fixed, his mouth may feel sore, and soft food is likely to be the order of the day. Give him some painkillers, and encourage him to apply some of the special wax the orthodontist supplies to any parts of the brace that seem to rub his mouth (and if the orthodontist does not offer any as a matter of course, ask for some). If that does not solve the problem pretty quickly, within a day or so, go back to the orthodontist for an adjustment. Braces are about correcting a smile – not medieval-strength torture! Taking a painkiller an hour before bedtime can be a good idea if an aching jaw is interfering with sleep.

CARING FOR A BRACE

There are some foods that you should avoid if you have braces. Raw chunks of carrot, whole apples, hard sweets, corn on the cob, sticky toffee and gum should be avoided, or the brackets may become dislodged. And braces are food magnets – they can get really grungy. Not only does this look gross, but the food that collects around the brackets can cause decay or staining. It is imperative that your teen cleans the area around the brackets thoroughly. Buy special brushes for this job, and a good mouthwash.

'When I look in the mirror I see the girl I was when I was growing up, with braces, crooked teeth, a baby face and a skinny body.'
HEATHER LOCKLEAR, actress

Defining idea...

How did it go?

Q **My daughter does not want braces, and refuses to go to the orthodontist. What can I do?**

A *It would be worth asking her why; if she has misconceptions, you (or the orthodontist) can allay her fears. If not, there is no point pushing her at this point. Keep a dialogue open, perhaps having her discuss the issue with other teens who wear braces. She may change her mind as she gets older. Give her plenty of information to make sure he can make an informed decision. You can collect leaflets and other information from the orthodontist or local dental hospital.*

Q **How long is my daughter likely to have to wear her brace?**

A *Most braces need to be worn for between six months and two years, but this varies according to the progress made. Your daughter will need to have regular checkups at the orthodontist, about every month or two. At each visit the orthodontist will check progress, and may adjust the braces to keep the pressure up on her teeth. After she has her braces removed, she will need to wear a retainer for a while to keep the teeth in position.*

42

Let's face it: acne anxieties

Many teens suffer from outbreaks of spots as their bodies experience hormonal upheaval.

But some teens suffer from acne — and it can make their life hell. How can you help?

Acne – severe, persisting outbreaks of angry red spots, blackheads and redness – is a skin condition suffered by a huge number of teenagers, and can be triggered by hormonal changes experienced during the teenage years. It is caused by the over activity of the sebaceous glands, which secrete an oily substance called sebum on to the skin. The face, back, chest, shoulders and upper arms can be affected.

Sebum can clog pores. Bacteria, normally present on the skin, thrive within the blocked pores, and cause an infection. The infection causes redness and swelling – a spot. Blackheads (comedones) may also be present. These are caused by a blockage of the pores, not by dirt. The dark colour is a reaction of material blocking the pores with the air. 'Whiteheads' are also common. These white fatty lumps are found just under the surface of the skin. They occur when excess sebum is trapped inside a hair follicle.

In severe inflammatory acne, cysts develop under the surface of the skin. These cysts can be painful to touch. They can rupture, and this may result in permanent scarring.

Acne can make your teenager totally miserable. She is feeling self conscious due to all the changes in her life, and this is made worse by the eruptions on her skin. Make sure that at the same time as she treats her skin, you bolster her self esteem. She may worry that no one will find her attractive. Reassure her that people are not that shallow, and she is still great to look at – she just has blemishes.

FIRST LINE OF DEFENCE – HOME TREATMENT

Be sensitive. Don't just say 'You are really spotty at the moment – would you like help?' or your daughter may run off to hide and whimper beneath the duvet. Perhaps say something along the lines of 'I can see that you are taking care of your skin, and I have seen some products that might help you.' All acne is not responsive to the same products, so she may need to experiment to find what works for her.

Be careful about the products she uses. Some are harsh and can cause redness and flaking. She should wash the affected area twice a day

Here's an idea for you...

Your teen – male or female – may want to use make up or tinted skin treatments to conceal spots. Consult your dermatologist for suggestions. The make up used – together with any moisturiser – should be water-based and labelled as 'non comedogenic'. That means it has been specially formulated so that it does not block pores (and cause comedones).

with a gentle, antibacterial cleanser or soap. Bear in mind that any cleansing regime may take weeks to show any effects, so she must be patient, hard though it is.

Try over-the-counter remedies available from the chemist. Benzoyl peroxide is the usual active ingredient; an antibacterial that dries the skin, encouraging it to shed the surface layer. This makes it less likely that pores will become blocked. The skin may become red and peel. Use the weakest lotion or cream first and work up to a stronger version after a couple of weeks if necessary.

Overwhelmed by the changes in your teen's life? Read IDEA 1, *All change here for the puberty express!*, for ways to cope.

Try another idea...

'Compliments invite the person who is complimented to embrace a new perception of him or herself. And just as layers and layers of nacre form a pearl over an irritating grain of sand, so compliments collect around us, developing us in all our beauty.'
DAPHNE ROSE KINGMA, author

Defining idea...

PRESCRIPTION MEDICINES

If the acne persists, visit your doctor. There are a variety of topical (applied to the skin) remedies as well as oral treatments. The doctor may prescribe antibiotic lotion to control the bacteria found on the skin. Topical retinoids may also be prescribed. These are based on vitamin A, and encourage the skin to peel. This lotion can make the skin sensitive to sunlight, so be careful.

Oral antibiotics may also be prescribed. These also kill off the bacteria infecting the skin, but a topical treatment will also need to be used to prevent the pores from becoming blocked. Improvement may take four to six months.

If the acne persists, consult a dermatologist. A dermatologist may prescribe Isotretinoin (marketed as Roaccutane). This is a powerful oral retinoid, used for the treatment of severe acne that has been resistant to other treatments. It dries oily skin secretions and has miraculous effects – but it should be considered carefully. My son took this drug and it was startlingly effective. There are, however, a number of side effects.

Isotretinoin is not suitable for people with liver or kidney disease. The skin may become dry and fragile, and there is an increased sensitivity to sunlight. Aches and pains in joints are common, as are headaches. Nosebleeds are common, and the lips may flake and bleed. The application of aqueous cream inside the nostrils and on the lips can help to reduce this. Isotretinoin can also cause damage to unborn babies, so girls must be sure not to become pregnant whilst taking the drug, and for several months afterwards. The drug has also been implicated as a cause of depression.

Q   **My son has a couple of severe acne scars. Will these ever go away or do they need treatment?**

How did it go?

A   *Scars will fade and flatten over time, but some are permanent. Scars caused by acne can be removed by dermabrasion, where layers of skin are rubbed away, or by laser treatment. Consult your dermatologist for more details.*

Q   **My son eats loads of junk food. Does it cause his acne?**

A   *No. There are many myths surrounding acne. It is not caused by bad hygiene, eating chocolate or junk food – it is caused by overactive seba-ceous glands. A less processed, varied diet that includes lots of fresh food and plenty of water will make him feel healthier, as will some regular exercise. That may make him feel better about himself, so his skin seems a less all encompassing issue. Don't link junk food with your teen's skin problems – your son will just get offended and you will be no further forward.*

43

Fast food and faddy diets

Teenagers are growing fast, and need to eat a full, healthy diet.

A healthy diet during adolescence is an important factor in helping to prevent diseases in adulthood such as obesity, anaemia, heart disease, osteoporosis and even cancer.

During adolescence, your child will have huge growth spurts. Bone density will also increase quickly for both boys and girls during this period. Teenagers require a healthy mixed diet rich in vitamins, carbohydrates, protein and essential fats to maintain their growth and health.

Teenagers should be getting about half of all their calories from slow burn complex carbohydrates such as bread, pasta, cereals and rice, and from fresh vegetables and fruit. About a third of their calories should come from protein rich foods such as milk, cheese, eggs, yoghurt, beans, tofu and meat. They also need healthy fats in their diet, so encourage them to eat nuts and oily fish.

Here's an idea for you… **Buy a smoothie maker, and encourage your teen to experiment. My teens love to create their own concoctions by hurling fruit, yogurts and juice into the machine. Some of the blends are an acquired taste, but they have made some great discoveries (clementine and mango or water melon and lime are particular favourites). A smoothie maker is better in health terms than a juicer as it keeps the fruit pulp in the mix – giving extra 'roughage', as your mother would have said. It makes eating '5 a day' so much easier!**

Of course, knowing what your teenage children should be eating and actually getting them to eat it are two different matters. They may have erratic eating patterns, and may often not actually be home at mealtimes as their schedule fills. They may skip breakfast for an extra few minutes in bed, or because they can't be bothered. They may also rebel about what you see as healthy food, and what they think they should be eating.

Your teen may associate 'junk' foods such as burgers, chips and other fast foods with fun and going out with friends. Whether he enjoys the food or not – and it is cheap and readily available – he will enjoy the context, and will continue to consume the food. Although fast food restaurants are making marketing forays into healthy eating options as a part of their regular menu, the main offerings are high fat and loaded with salt.

Before you try to change your teenager's eating habits, look at your own. Remember, he will sniff out hypocrisy a mile off. Do you miss breakfast and grab a fatty pastry snack mid morning? Do you have a handful of nuts and dried fruit mid afternoon – or a bar of chocolate to boost your flagging energy levels? Your teens are watching you …

If your teen comes food shopping with you, encourage him to become a knowledgeable shopper – that doesn't just mean evaluating the best deals; it also means developing the habit of label reading. If he realises that the sugary snacks he wants to pile in the trol-

Worried your teen is eating an unhealthy diet? Read IDEA 44, *A weighty issue*, for tips on coping with extra pounds.

Try another idea...

ley are full of all manner of artificial colours and additives, he may be less keen on them. Explain why you don't want to buy certain foods – and you favour others. 'Because they are good/bad for you' just won't cut it any more – he needs explanations. Encourage him to do his own research on various ingredients – he will be amazed, and those healthy snacks may just become more attractive!

Your teen's attitudes to food, size and weight are learned at home, and a healthy attitude is important for their lifelong health. (No pressure there then …!) Be a good role model. If you are a constant dieter, or you make jokes about heavy people, you are sending the message that thin is better. Resist the urge to talk in terms of 'good' and 'bad' food – it's just food. In moderation, the fattiest and most sugary treats are fine – as long as the rest of the diet is well balanced.

MEAT IS MURDER...

If your teen agrees with Morrissey, you may have to learn about vegetarian cookery. My teens are veggies so it comes as second nature to me. It is important that vegetarian teens get all the nutrients they need to stay healthy. Cutting meat out of a diet is fine, but it needs to be replaced with an alternative such as

'The wise man should consider that health is the greatest of human blessings. Let food be your medicine.'

HIPPOCRATES

Defining idea...

quorn, soya, pulses and nuts – and if your child is not vegan, with dairy products and eggs. A vitamin supplement especially formulated for vegetarians is a good idea to smooth over the transition.

How did it go?

Q **I cleaned out my 14-year-old daughter's school bag and found a couple of mouldy packed lunches. She said she just prefers to get a bag of chips at lunchtime. How can I make lunches she will actually eat?**

A *Talk to your daughter – she may have ideas of her own. Try alternatives such as pastry vegetable wraps and stuffed pittas. Add cheese chunks and vegetable sticks with dips made from soft cheese or yoghurt mixed with onion and spices. Add a drink of juice or a smoothie instead of fizzy drinks. Even if your daughter does eat fatty, less nutritious snacks at lunchtime, don't forget you can make up for it at dinner time with a balanced meal – it's overall nutrition that matters, rather than what she eats at each individual meal.*

Q **My teen never takes any exercise. She's always in front of the TV or on the computer talking to friends. How can I encourage her to be more active?**

A *Many teens – especially girls – give up sport in favour of 'hanging out' at this stage. Often, girls give up sport and never start again. Your daughter needs to find an exercise she enjoys. Exercise will help to make your teen feel good about her body, and may raise her self esteem as well as her heart rate! If she does not like team sports, she may enjoy running, kickboxing or Kendo.*

44

A weighty issue

Obesity is reaching epidemic proportions in the western world, with associated ill health costing millions.

Health implications aside, being overweight can make your teen feel isolated and unattractive.

Like adults, teenagers become overweight when they overeat, consuming more food than their body needs. Obese adolescents are very likely to become obese adults. The health risks are enormous. Obesity can lead to the development of diabetes, liver, heart and respiratory problems, and orthopaedic problems as excess weight stresses joints. There are also emotional problems associated with obesity. Teenagers who are – or perceive themselves to be – overweight can suffer from low self esteem. Their peer group may tease or bully them for being overweight – and thus, different from the herd.

Magazines aimed at teens feature waifish models. TV shows aimed at teenagers tend to show slim, 'beautiful' people – unless they are comedies, when there may be a larger character playing it for laughs. All this can lead to a very unhappy over-weight teenager.

Here's an idea for you...

Ensure your teenager eats a nutritious breakfast such as a whole wheat or oat cereal, or eggs (boiled or poached) on toast. He may prefer fruit, yoghurt and a home made muffin. It's easy to whip up the muffin batter in the food processor the night before and you can leave it in the pans in the oven to turn on as you switch on the kettle. Add a handful of wheatgerm plus blackcurrants or blueberries to the mixture and you have super tasty, warm breakfast goods with little effort. Add a glass of juice or milk and your teen is set up for the day. This will prevent him from feeling listless mid morning and reaching for a high sugar snack for a burst of energy.

WHAT CAUSES OBESITY?

Obese teens overeat – and what they eat tends to be high in fat and sugar. 'Glands' do not tend to be responsible, although genetics can. It is thought that a genetic predisposition to obesity comes into play in 25–40% of cases of teenage obesity.

Low levels of activity also contribute. Watching TV, computer gaming and even homework are all sedentary occupations. Many teens are ferried about in cars rather than walking places. If your teen does not take part in any active exercise, this will obviously contribute to her weight gain. If she is very stressed, perhaps by exam or relationship pressure, she may binge eat which can also lead to massive weight gain.

The whole culture of eating has changed, which means as a society we are getting fatter. The overall cost of food has decreased in relation to earnings. Food is readily available and can be cheap to buy, especially poor quality food. Aggressively marketed (and often aimed at teenagers) energy-dense foods and drinks are available everywhere, from petrol stations to supermarkets. Portion sizes of these foods have increased, with 'king size' confectionery bars and massive bags of snacks being the norm.

Concerned about the possibility of eating disorders? Take a look at IDEA 45, *Body image blues*, to find out more.

Try another idea…

More food is prepared away from home for convenience as fewer families have a stay-at-home parent. Many teens are unable to cook meals from scratch as they have rarely seen it done at home as convenience and pre-prepared, processed foods become commonplace.

HOW CAN I HELP MY TEEN TO MAINTAIN A HEALTHY WEIGHT?

Weight loss programs or diets are not really effective with this age group. You should be careful to make your teenage child feel good about herself, and not feel that you disapprove of her weight; this could be very damaging to her self image. She needs

'I've been on a diet for two weeks and all I've lost is two weeks.'

TOTIE FIELDS, comedienne

Defining idea…

193

nutritional advice, combined with a change in her attitude to food and a more active lifestyle.

Healthy eating strategies should include the whole family. Changing what is available in the cupboards will help to avoid 'mooching', where your teen trawls the cupboards looking for tasty (but high sugar and fat) treats such as crisps and confectionery.

Make sure that when you go shopping you buy plenty of healthy snacks, such as yoghurts, exotic fruit, and ingredients for low fat home made dips (whiz together low fat yoghurt or fromage frais with chives, onions and spices).

Don't buy soft drinks; even the low sugar varieties are loaded with chemicals and encourage a sweet tooth. Encourage your teens to drink plenty of water, carbonated or still. Emphasise the skin benefits if they need encouragement!

Watch portion sizes of energy-dense, nutrient-poor foods such as desserts, confectionery and salty high fat snacks. That roughly translates to 'a little of what you fancy does you good; a lot just makes you overweight'. Banishing ice cream, chocolate and chips completely will just make your teen want them more as they become 'forbidden foods'.

Q   **I have noticed that my son regularly buys huge slabs of chocolate when he has a heavy study workload. He is starting to gain weight quite quickly and has complained about it. How can I help him?**

How did it go?

A   *Apart from implementing a healthy eating routine at mealtimes, try to help him to break the link between emotions and food. Change his focus of 'comfort eating' if he is miserable; suggest a fun outing together such as the cinema instead. Encourage him to take study breaks and go for a walk with you (and the dog!) – it will help clear his head and offers some 'chatting time' when he can air any problems he is having.*

Q   **I grew up in a house where you could not leave the table until you cleared your plate. When my teen doesn't finish the nutritious meals I cook for him, I worry he will fill up on fatty snacks later. Should I encourage him to eat everything I put in front of him?**

A   *If your teen doesn't finish his dinner, don't fuss. Allow him to be in touch with his own natural appetite – something modern adults find hard to gauge and a contributory factor in the obesity epidemic. Be careful about the snacks you have in the fridge and cupboards and 'empty nutrition snacks' are less likely to be a problem.*

45

Body image blues

Teenagers are often insecure, uncertain and uncomfortable in their own changing bodies.

It is perhaps not surprising that many of them develop an unhealthy body image, and this can lead in some cases to eating disorders.

Teenagers, like all of us, are bombarded daily with media images of stick thin models with perfect skin and hair. Magazines, TV programmes and newspapers give off one message – thin is in. Teenagers are more likely to feel insecure and crave the 'ideal' appearance than older adults. Explain to your teen that the average girl or boy does not look like a model – in fact, the models in magazines are not as 'perfect' as they look; they are airbrushed into 'perfection'.

Talk to your teens about the images they see, and deconstruct them. Talk about why thin and waifish is seen as attractive. Look at other images of beauty. Discuss the images seen as desirable, and talk about the way in which people – sometimes painfully and at great expense – reshape their bodies to conform to a false ideal.

Talk about peer pressure to be thin. What sort of 'diet culture' is your teen subjected to at school? She may feel left out if she is not as skinny as others and may

Here's an idea for you...

Be a healthy role model. If you are constantly on a diet, you are setting your growing child a bad example. He will learn that his weight is something to obsess about. Likewise, if you make jokes about your teen being chubby, you are giving him the message that thinner is better. Avoid making comments about body size – yours, his, or anyone else's for that matter.

feel under pressure to diet. Teenagers can be cruel, and their comments and taunts can drive non conformists into an isolated, depressed state. This can lead to an eating disorder as your teen strives to be like the others. If she constantly strives to attain a weight and shape that is not natural to her body, she will feel dissatisfied with herself. Make sure that she knows that she is beautiful, and help her to see that she does not have to conform to some waiflike or 'Barbie' ideal for people to like her. Make real efforts to boost her self esteem, giving her genuine compliments about how lustrous her hair is, how amusing she is, what a loyal friend she is etc. Make sure you promote a sensible attitude towards food and eating at home. Encourage your child to eat a healthy diet with plenty of fruit, whole grains and vegetables, but don't talk about food in terms of it being 'good', 'bad' or 'naughty' – it's just food. Make mealtimes relaxed; a time when the family catches up with the news of the day. If there are tensions, this can make any food anxieties worse.

HOW DO I RECOGNISE AN EATING DISORDER?

Anorexia nervosa

If your teen is suffering from anorexia, she has a distorted body image. She may be thin, but she sees herself as fat and will starve herself. She may wear loose clothes to disguise her weight loss.

Your teenager may skip family meals, possibly saying she has already eaten. She may eat bulky but low-calorie food, such as celery or lettuce.

She may have abdominal pains after eating as her stomach shrinks. She may also suffer from constipation, but it is likely that any laxatives she takes may be to rid her body of food rather than to remedy the problem. If her weight drops dramatically before puberty, her periods may be delayed. If she has started menstruating, her periods may stop. Her skin and nails may become very dry and fragile. Your teen may exercise excessively, but she is likely to feel weak and tired due to lack of adequate nutrition.

Worried your teen is under pressure? Check out IDEA 50, *Distress or de-stress?*, for ways to help.

Try another idea…

Seek professional help as soon as you can if you suspect anorexia – it is a potentially fatal illness. Consult your doctor in the first instance. She may recommend a specialist clinic.

Offer support and encouragement to your teen but approach it with delicacy. Your teen is suffering from a mental illness, and she may feel that her weight is the only area of her life that she can control. She may therefore be resistant to getting treatment which she may feel will undermine her.

Bulimia nervosa

If your teen is bulimic, she may not appear overly thin. If she is bulimic, she may regularly indulge in binge eating. Large quantities of fatty, sweet foods are eaten in a short time, usually in secret. After a binge, she is likely

'Take care of your body. It's the only place you have to live.'

JIM ROHN, author and motivational speaker

Defining idea…

199

to feel a sense of guilt and she will purge the food from her system by vomiting, or taking laxatives. She may also take diuretics. Repeated vomiting will deprive your teen of nutrients and salts. She may have dry, puffy skin, and swollen glands in her face and neck. She may damage her digestive system and throat, and even start to vomit blood. Her teeth will suffer as a result of regular exposure to stomach acids.

Once again, seek medical help as soon as possible if you suspect bulimia.

How did it go?

Q **I keep finding sweet wrappers and empty packets from fatty foods in the bin. My daughter doesn't eat with us either, and she's very slim. Where do the calories go – could it be bulimia?**

A *It could be – but not necessarily. Parents of bulimics may find that high fat foods disappear from the cupboard; they may find food or wrappers hidden in cupboards or bins. On the other hand, your child may just not be eating with you due to scheduling clashes – or because she doesn't want to. As a result she may be snacking regularly. Watch out for other signs of bulimia such as vomiting smells, heavy use of scented sprays in the bathroom etc.*

Q **Are teens more likely to suffer from eating disorders?**

A *Anorexia mainly affects girls between the ages of 14 and 25, but it is also becoming more common amongst boys. Bulimia is most likely in girls between the ages of 13 and 27 but young male athletes may also develop bulimia as they become fixated on their body image.*

46

Evil stepmonster or big bad teen?

Stepfamilies have had bad press for centuries. From the wicked stepmothers and foul stepsisters of classic fairy tales to the battling stepfamilies seen in TV soaps, blended families are often portrayed in a less than glowing light.

You may have fallen in love with your new partner — but that doesn't mean your respective children have fallen in love with each other — or with their new step-parent! There are things you can do, however, to smooth the transition, as your families merge.

The closeness demanded by living in a shared household can be incredibly difficult to cope with when the people sharing the home have suddenly arrived – and the

Here's an idea for you... **You need time in each other's company to feel comfortable – let alone to feel like members of a new, happy family unit! Make sure you eat meals together regularly, and have outings and activities such as visits to the cinema. You need to build a sense of belonging together, and that cannot be rushed or created falsely.**

teenagers involved may well be hostile to the new arrangements. The stresses of ordinary family life are magnified, and the strain can cause upset and conflict. The teenagers in both families may feel that they wish everything could return to the days when there were two separate families, before the first parental relationships broke down. If your split from your previous partner was acrimonious, your child may feel torn. If you were the partner who instigated the break in the first relationship – and especially if you were having an affair with the new step-parent – your teen may feel guilty if he gets on with his new step-parent and even feel that he is betraying his other birth parent. This is especially true if your ex is still reeling from the relationship break-up. Alternatively, he may yearn for the time when he lived with one parent, and didn't have to share him or her.

New stepbrothers or stepsisters can be perceived as invaders. Teenagers are creatures of habit, and they find anything that upsets the status quo threatening. If a new step-parent or siblings move into your family home, this can feel like an invasion of their 'safe space.' Add these feelings to a new set of family rules, habits and expectations and the outcome can be explosive. Don't try to rush your children into accepting the new situation, and avoid other changes at the same time if possible. Coping with a blended family and moving at the same time is incredibly difficult. It may look like a fresh start to you, but it may mean losing important sources of support to your teenage child – friends, school teachers and relatives that live nearby. Talk through any suggested move carefully with your teens and find out their views before committing yourself, and be prepared to compromise. It will save you a lot of heartache in the long run.

Finding it hard to connect with the teens in your life? Read IDEA 14, *Making time*, for tips on improving the situation.

Try another idea...

YOU'RE NOT MY DAD!

Flashpoints can occur where you and your new partner have different attitudes to parenting. If you are laissez faire in your attitude, and your new partner is more of a disciplinarian, the fur is sure to fly! Attempts to assert authority over stepchildren, before you have built a relationship with them is just plain foolhardy. Even once you have been accepted, it can be a bone of contention and must be handled with sensitivity. It does not take much provocation for a teenager to point out that you are not *really* his parent …

You are *not* a substitute mother or father, nor should you try to be. God forbid you should cheesily exhort him to see you 'as a friend,' but present yourself as another adult who is available to offer him care and support.

'To be sure a stepmother to a girl is a different thing to a second wife to a man!'
ELIZABETH GASKELL,
author and philanthropist

Defining idea...

203

Discuss any problems fully with your partner to avoid friction between the pair of you, and be guided by their views – they know their children best, and can guide you on the usual family response to infractions. That does not mean your views cannot be taken into account; it does mean that they will be tempered – and ultimately sanctioned – by your partner, who is the 'natural' parent.

EASING THE TRANSITION

All families are different, but there are strategies you can use to smooth over the worst wrinkles as your newly shaped family is formed.

- Give it time. Be realistic, and don't try to force people to get along.
- Encourage your teen to talk about feelings and problems, rather than bottling things up. Listen carefully and do not react angrily. If your teen is acting badly, it is as a result of his emotional turmoil.
- Make sure each child has some privacy and his own space
- Make sure you spend some time with your 'natural child', one-to-one.
- Create new family traditions for special occasions such as Christmas or birthdays. This can include blended family traditions – or you can invent totally new ones.

Q **My daughter complains incessantly about her stepfather – who is trying his best. What can I do to help?**

How did it go?

A *Listen carefully and stay calm. Do not react angrily, as your teenager may feel you are being disloyal and taking your partner's side. You cannot make your daughter like your new partner, and only time and good communication will help her to work her feelings through. Insist, however, on an atmosphere of mutual respect. Make sure you support your partner and let him know you appreciate his efforts – he will be having a hard time adjusting too.*

Q **My teens and my partner's 17-year-old seem to loathe each other and there are daily rows. What can I do?**

A *Listen to both sides, and try to find the main triggers for the rows. Talk to your partner, and then all sit down together to discuss the situation. State firmly that you live together and must find a way to get on. Make a list of the things that cause the most friction, and deal with them. Time will smooth out the underlying strangeness of the situation, but you can deal with the trigger points such as privacy and sharing time to help things along.*

47

Labelling is disabling: giving your teen a bad name

If you keep telling your teenagers what they are, there is every danger they will live up to the labels and become what you say – for better or for worse!

So be careful how you describe them ...

Were you the brainy one? Was your sister the beauty? Perhaps you were the clumsy one, the clown or the sporty one. Families create roles for their children, usually unwittingly or by accident. These roles can become self fulfilling prophecies, where a child grows up internalising the role assigned – whether it really fits or not. Think about it for a moment. Listen to what your siblings and parents say about you. Think about your nicknames, and the stories about you that have entered family folklore (usually told with an indulgent laugh, at times guaranteed to create maximum embarrassment): 'Do you remember when you were a bridesmaid for Aunty Helen and got tangled up with the cat in her veil? You always were the clumsy one – but the pictures were *so* cute!'

Family members are cast into roles and are given shiny – and often indelible – labels to match. These labels quickly become part of your child's self image, and can be

Here's an idea for you…

When you are talking to your teen, divorce behaviour from 'self'. That means you criticise the *behaviour* you find unacceptable, rather than your teen – and that avoids labelling her. For example, if she leaves the bathroom looking like a swamp, don't call her a slob; tell her she needs to pick up after herself instead of expecting other people to do it.

hard to shake off. If you see your teenage son as a klutz, he may see himself as such – and become nervous about breaking things. These nerves may actually lead to him having accidents – and reinforce the idea that he is clumsy.

Even positive labels can be damaging. If you constantly refer to your son as 'sensible', he may feel he has to live up to that expectation, and miss out on spontaneity and fun, as his label inhibits him. He may worry that if you ever realise that he is not always 'sensible', you may be disappointed in him. Likewise, if you take obvious pride in his sporting ability, that's fine. But if you seem to define him in terms of his sporting ability, ignoring the other facets of his personality, you are labelling him. He may feel that you will be horribly disappointed if he does not perform well, and feel diminished in your eyes. This can lead to real emotional difficulties and a strained relationship.

Make sure that you have not unwittingly attached a label to your teen to fulfil your own emotional needs. For example, if you see your daughter as hopelessly disorganised, ask yourself if you like having to organise her life to make you feel needed. If there's a truth in this, encourage her to be more independent – and buy yourself a dog!

Baffled by your teen's appearance – relax! Read IDEA 16, *Punk princess or just plain peculiar?*, to see why it's normal...

Try another idea...

HOW TO UNTIE YOUR TEEN'S LABEL

Just because a certain type of behaviour has persisted for a long time, it does not mean it is a personality trait. You can help your teen to see himself in a different way, and gently help him to change his behaviour. Catch him being 'good', and reinforce socially helpful behaviour with praise. Don't gush he will see through you in a second.

Some teens label themselves – and the labels can be damning. They may see themselves as unpopular, shy, untidy – whatever the internal label, you can help them to get out of the habit by deprogramming their ideas. If they make a self deprecating remark, counter it. If they say, 'I can't do that, I'm too shy,' remind them of a time they have been bold.

Defining idea...

'**Labelling is for suits – not people. Once we try to define people and attach a handy label to describe them, we are in danger of moulding them into our image of them. Once we try to mould them, we may be forcing them to take on a shape that does not fit. This force deforms the spirit.'**

EMILY PICKLES, author

How did it go?

Q **Surely labelling my teen can't be that harmful? She is a bit of a dizzy creature, and she knows it. It's part of what makes her loveable!**

A *Defining your teen in this way is potentially harmful. She may live up to her label in order to conform to your expectations. Her label may influence the way others respond and behave towards her – and this will push her towards being 'dizzy'.*

  Research has shown that students identified by their teacher at the beginning of the academic year as 'slow' or 'gifted' learners will tend to perform at the level of their label by the end of the year – frighteningly – regardless of their actual ability. The students live up to their label. This may be true of your daughter too. If you – and others – treat her according to her label, she may well live up to them as part of a self-fulfilling prophecy. Don't let your thinking and responses to your daughter be coloured by the label you have assigned to her – just give her a chance to be herself!

Q **My family always referred to me as the 'brainy' one. It sounds great – but I lived in fear of not living up to their expectations, and letting them down. How can I avoid that with my own teenage son?**

A *It is great to be praised, but you are right to be concerned about the way that expectations can be hard to live up to. Let your son know you see him as bright and talented – but let him know that you love him for himself – not for his skills and talents. Let him see that you make mistakes and be a good role model – don't be too hard on yourself.*

48

Safe as houses: teaching your teen about personal safety

As you release your teenage child into the big bad world you worry about her safety – you are a parent; it comes with the territory.

There are things you can teach her in order to help her to stay safe — so take heart!

It is important to teach your teen, before she is out and about on her own on a regular basis, the fundamentals of staying safe. Building on the road safety and stranger danger lessons you taught her as a younger child, these skills will last her for the rest of her life.

Teenagers may become victims of crime because they can easily be led into dangerous situations; they may indulge in risky behaviour because they feel invulnerable. Making your teens more aware of the risks they face will help them to stay out of danger. You will not always be there to keep them safe, so you need to equip them with tools, such as problem solving skills and clear decision making abilities.

STRATEGIES FOR STAYING SAFE

- Make sure your teenager has an understanding of situations to avoid, such as accepting lifts from people she does not know, hitchhiking or accepting lifts when friends have been drinking etc.
- Encourage your teenager to listen to her own feelings and intuitions. Once she senses difficulties or danger, she needs to be confident enough to act upon them. This is harder than it sounds for your teenager – she may be afraid of looking stupid in front of her friends.
- When your teen is walking alone, especially at night, she should stay alert and aware of her surroundings and situation. This includes keeping her personal stereo turned off, and not walking along chatting on her mobile phone.
- Encourage her to stick to busy roads which are well lit – avoiding quiet short cuts and alleyways.
- If she thinks someone is following her, she should cross the road and go somewhere busy such as an occupied bus stop, or a shop. If houses are nearby, she should walk purposefully to a door and ring the bell.
- When travelling alone by bus, your teen should learn to sit forwards, near the driver, and use bus stops on busy roads.
- Encourage your child to carry a personal alarm or a whistle.

Here's an idea for you… **Take a self-defence course together. If your teenager is willing to put in the work and practice a few exercises, a self defence class can be very valuable. Knowing how to get out of a hold, how to use pressure points and how to kick, bite or hit to escape from an assailant is invaluable knowledge. Learning a few simple moves rather than lots of complex strategies is better as your teen may forget the complex ones in a crisis.**

- Teach your teen to keep valuables such as mobile phones and personal stereos in pockets or bags out of sight.
- Make sure your teen knows that she should not fight if someone tries to rob her; it is better to concentrate on memorising the details of an attacker's appearance.
- Encourage your teenager to keep a safe distance from situations that can become difficult, and make her feel uncomfortable, such as heavy drinking, acting offensively towards others etc.
- Make sure that if your teen is drinking alcohol, she is careful to stay in control; she should also keep a close eye on her drinks to avoid them being spiked.

Worried because it's time to let go? Read IDEA 49, *Fly free, my pretties!*, to release your teen from your clutches with grace.

Try another idea…

SEXUAL SAFETY

Your teenager needs to know that if another person is overfamiliar, does not respect her personal space or touches her when uninvited that she should say no with force, looking the offender in the eye, and then seek help from a person in a position of authority such as a parent, teacher or law enforcement officer.

Encourage your teen to understand that she has a right to say no to any sexual advances that she does not want – and that includes the knowledge that it is OK to kiss and cuddle without having sex; she must be confident enough to not be coerced into having sex.

If the worst happens and your teen is sexually assaulted, needs to know that she can trust

'Safety is something that happens between your ears, not something you hold in your hands.'
JEFF COOPER, editor *Guns and Ammo* magazine

Defining idea…

213

you to help her. Make sure she knows that she will be believed, and no blame will be attached to her for the attack – whatever she is wearing, wherever she has been, she has the right to say no and be listened to. The only blame should be firmly laid at the door of the attacker.

Make sure your teenager has the right attitude to deflect an attack. That means recognising and utilising anger at being attacked. Many people freeze in a frightening situation, and this stops them from thinking logically. If you encourage your teenager to channel her anger, to think 'this is not fair – I do *not* deserve this' she is more likely to think and act quickly and decisively, and thus avoid harm.

How did it go?

Q **Is it important to teach boys about safety – or is it a 'girl thing'?**

A *These strategies should be taught to both girls and boys – remember, teenage boys are the most likely victims of violent crime.*

Q **My son is going to college this year and will be living in a rented flat. What can I do to help him to keep safe?**

A *Once your teen leaves home to go to college, he faces a new set of challenges and dangers. If he is living in halls of residence he is less likely to be burgled than in a privately rented house or flat, but he should still be careful to mark his possessions and lock up carefully. If he is living in a flat of his own, you should help him to fit window locks and deadlocks on doors if possible. Make sure he is adequately insured, and encourage him to bring valuables home during the holidays. Buy him a timer switch to turn on lights, radios etc. when he is away.*

49

Fly free, my pretties!

As a parent, you want to nurture strong teenagers that can stand on their own, so you can be confident they will survive out in the world at large.

But actually setting them 'free' can be harder than you could possibly imagine ...

It is natural that you feel protective towards your children and want to keep them safe. This is the same for the parent of teens as it is for the parents of toddlers. The stakes change as they grow up and move further out into the world, away from the shelter of the family.

As the parent of a small child, you were a powerful figure. You knew the minutiae of your child's life; he listened to your instructions and you felt in control. You made all the decisions. As he grew, he moved away from you, listening instead to his friends and peers. He routinely challenged your authority, and resisted most attempts to control his life.

Now the time has come for him to take his place in the world as an adult. By leaving home to go to university, or to travel on a gap year, or to start work, he is moving even further from your sphere of protection. This can be a very worrying time for you as you wonder if he can really cope alone.

As your child prepares to move away from home, make sure that along with the IKEA kitchenware and bedding, she takes posters, throws and other items to make her room feel more like home. Help her to draw up a budget, and buy her a simple cook book. Talk about how you coped when you first moved out of your parents' home. Encourage other family members or friends to talk about their experiences. Stick to the positives, but prepare her for the negatives, such as feeling homesick. Send her little parcels of goodies – including phonecards for her mobile phone, so she can keep in touch – so she has a taste of home.

Think about it for a moment. He has taken exams, and organised his workload. He has learned how to set – and achieve – goals and meet deadlines. He should by now have shown himself to be reliable in terms of coping with a part time job, going away without you on holiday, and organising his social life. Although he may seem feckless at times – running out of money, leaving his room in a state, leaving dirty laundry about the house – he is likely to cope in a very different way when he has to. That's the rub for many parents. If you pick up the slack and give him more money when he runs out, instead of helping him to budget, he will not learn to take care of himself. If you rush to his bedroom to find dirty laundry, then sort, wash and iron it, he will not learn to look after his own clothes. Despite appearances, he is a capable person, equipped for taking care of himself. It is likely that he only appears disorganised and at times helpless because you give him too much support. Once you are not there, he may find the early days hard work, but he will survive after a sharp learning curve – like all young home leavers!

GOING TO UNIVERSITY

Your teen has been clamouring for more freedom for some time. If he is going to university, this is his chance! The move into halls of residence or a student flat is the perfect opportunity for him to get a taste of independent life in a structured way, with the opportunity to return home for the long holidays for a bit of pampering!

However, the reality may be less exciting – and more worrying – than your teen would like to admit. He may not want to admit that he is anxious about leaving home, so talk about university in a general way, giving him a chance to voice any concerns. He may be uneasy about having to meet a totally new group of people, and making new friends. He may be worried as well as excited about living away from home, and may be concerned about the course he has chosen. He may be worried about whether he has chosen the right course, or if he is up to the academic work.

You may feel anxious about your teenager's move too. Hold on to the idea that he is a capable person, and remember all of the things you have taught him. He is not helpless! Remember too – you left home once, and you survived to tell the tale. Reassure him – and yourself – that if he needs help, you are always just a phone call, text or email away.

Read about ways to keep your teen safe as she spreads her wings in IDEA 48, *Safe as houses: teaching your teen about personal safety.*

Try another idea...

'There are only two lasting bequests we can hope to give our children. One is roots; the other, wings.'
CARTER HODDING, journalist and publisher

Defining idea...

How did
it go?

Q **My teenage daughter is worried that she may not like the course she has chosen at university as she has not studied it before, and I am doing my best to reassure her. Do you think it is perhaps a case of nerves?**

A *Your daughter may well be nervous, especially if she has chosen a subject she has not studied before. Encourage her to read some of the set books before she starts the course, to set her mind at rest. Her choice is not irreversible, if she finds she really does not like it, and it is possible to change – but encourage her to give the course a chance before she makes any hasty choices.*

Q **My daughter has just started university, and is very homesick. What can I do to make her feel better – should I tell her to come home each weekend?**

A *Your daughter will probably settle more quickly if she stays there for the first few weeks – she needs to meet people to make friends! Keep in touch via instant messenger, text and phone and send packages of goodies with notes from family and friends tucked in along with the treats.*

50

Distress or de-stress?

It might be hard to believe, looking at your teenager as she lies slumped on the sofa – but she is subject to an immense amount of stress.

Give your teens an invaluable lesson that will last a lifetime, by helping them to develop strategies to cope with stress – starting with the adult responsibilities that land on teenage shoulders.

Teenagers, in the same way as adults, experience stress everyday. Apart from general large scale sources of stress, such as divorce of parents, illness, bereavement and moving house, teenagers have specific areas that cause immense stress – and they occur largely because they are teenagers.

School or college may be a source of stress, especially around exam time. You can unwittingly increase your teen's stress levels by having expectations that are unreasonably high for her; this can set her up to feel a failure when she does not achieve the grades you expect. Coursework can also put a strain on teenagers as

Here's an idea for you... **Help your teen to reprogramme himself. If his internal soundtrack includes lots of negative self talk such as 'I am stupid; I'll never be able to do this work', encourage him to come up with neutral or positive alternatives such as 'I am finding this really hard right now. I need to find myself a study buddy or get help from a faculty member to help me to understand.'**

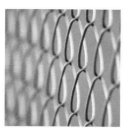

they struggle with a large number of examination courses, the coursework and homework associated. Add to this the demands of extra curricular activities – important these days, not just for fun, but to build a CV and college applications – and your teenager can quickly reach saturation point.

Your teenager may also experience stress due to problems with friends, and peer pressure. Teenage friendship groups can be volatile and capricious and your teen may find herself being treated as flavour of the month one day and then be excluded from group activities for no apparent reason the next. This can be crushing, so take it seriously. Try to remember yourself what it was like when you were a teenager and you felt excluded from an activity – it hurts. Peer pressure may give her a huge amount of stress, especially as it comes into conflict with the mores she has grown up with. She may feel torn as she knows that certain behaviour – drinking, sexual activity, smoking etc. – will cause trouble at home, but her lack of participation may mark her as an outsider, or 'childish'. Even when she does not want to take part in an activity, she will be under pressure to conform, and this can be hard to bear for even the strongest minded teen.

Your teen will also experience stress due to her self image. Her body is undergoing huge changes and that is hard to come to terms with and can cause stress in itself. Dealing with associated irritations such as spots and acne and sexual development including the onset of periods can be uniquely stressful. Negative thoughts and low self image can be a problem for your teen if she feels that she does not conform to the image of beauty prevalent in the media – especially that aimed at teens. If she is not willowy, with clear skin and lustrous hair, she may feel unattractive.

It is easy to see how your teen can become overloaded with stress, and how it can take over her life. If unmanaged, stress can cause depression, aggressive or risky behaviour and physical illness. Your teen may be unaware of how the stress she is experiencing can affect her behaviour, but you will know! You should monitor your teen's stress levels and try to intervene when necessary

There does seem to be a gender difference in teens dealing with stress. Your stressed son may ignore his problems, throwing himself

Look at IDEA 3, *Too much pressure*, to find ways to help your teen cope with pressure.

Try another idea...

Defining idea...

'**Stress is basically a disconnection from the earth, a forgetting of the breath. Stress is an ignorant state. It believes that everything is an emergency. Nothing is that important. Just lie down.**'
NATALIE GOLDBERG, author

into a fury of sporting or social activities, although he may identify stress triggers and problems and meet them head on. Your stressed daughter is more likely to talk about problems with her friends, which can be a great strategy – but if the stress is caused by problems with her friendship group, this can cause even more problems as she may feel isolated and cut off from her usual coping mechanisms and strategies.

HOW YOU CAN HELP

Just being aware of the stress triggers your teenager faces is a great start. Watch for the signs and keep lines of communication open. Help her to work out solutions to particular problems to alleviate stress, and to develop a range of practical coping skills, such as breaking large tasks into smaller manageable chunks. If she is feeling overwhelmed by the thought of exams, help her to work out a revision timetable. If she is regularly feeling left out by friends, encourage her to develop new friendships, perhaps by joining groups associated with hobbies or interests.

Encourage your teen to take exercise and eat regular, nutritious meals. It sounds like a simplistic response, but it helps. She is less likely to feel run down if she is eating properly and the exercise will help to clear her head so she gains perspective on her problems. She should avoid too much caffeine as this can make her feel jumpy and agitated. Taking a break from stressful situations by chatting to a friend on the phone, taking the dog for a walk or listening to CDs can help, as can relaxation exercises. Breathing deeply from her abdomen will help to loosen tight muscles and release tension.

Q   **My son is very hard on himself – a complete perfectionist. How can I help him?**

How did it go?

A   *Apart from general stress relief, encourage your son to feel satisfied with doing a 'good enough' job for many tasks, especially less important ones rather than going for perfection every time.*

Q   **Is it worth trying alternative therapies?**

A   *Absolutely. Consider aromatherapy, using a diffuser to fill the house with calming scents. Indian head massage may help to ease tension, and homeopathic remedies to calm stress. Rescue Remedy is a very useful aid for a quick response to stress, and your teen can carry some in his bag in readiness.*

   There are many very helpful therapies to explore. Check what is avail-able locally, and find out more about each therapy online before your teen decides which he would like to try.

Nobody understands me ...

Teenage depression can blight lives. But recognising the problem is the first step to dealing with it and making your teenager feel better.

How to tell the difference between ordinary teenage angst and depression in your teenager — and how to help.

One of the main problems with depression is that the symptoms can be subtle and the early signs may be easy to miss. This is even more the case with teenagers who can be very moody and anti social at times. Your teenager may feel down or even depressed for a variety of reasons – or for no tangible or apparent reason at all.

IDENTIFYING DEPRESSION IN YOUR TEEN – SIGNS TO WATCH OUT FOR

Your teen may be suffering from depression if he experiences some of these problems:

- He seems to be listless and has no energy.
- He feels anxious and finds it hard to think clearly.
- He feels like a failure.
- He feels hopeless and useless; he sees no future.
- Social activity is avoided – he feels anxious and unable to function socially.

- Even small tasks feel impossible to manage.
- Sleeping may be disturbed – either insomnia or long stretches of sleeping.
- He may be off his food or may 'comfort eat'.
- He may be more irritable than usual and have mood swings.
- He may have aches and pains that have no obvious physical causes.
- He may feel victimised, or that life is unfair.
- He may feel very self critical.

HOW YOU CAN HELP

It can be difficult to communicate with your teen if he is depressed, but you must not ignore his feelings in the hope that things will improve of their own accord. You must let him know that you care about the way he feels and will support him. He will be feeling confused and scared, and your intervention and involvement is vital.

Above all, you must be willing to really listen to your teenager. Let him know that he does not have to cope alone, and that he has your unconditional love. Do not be tempted to minimise his concerns; even if they sound unreasonable to you, they are very real to him. He already feels no one understands and this increases his feelings of isolation.

Ask questions, but do not be pushy, or nag in your desire to 'get to the bottom' of the problem. He will feel threatened and cornered, and is likely to close up. Try to reassure him. Share your own feelings, and let him know that everyone, including you, feels down or even depressed at times. If you have been

Here's an idea for you... **Encourage your teenager to do the things she enjoys, and invite her out on small outings such as for a coffee or for a walk – but don't be offended if she does not want to come at first. Keep things simple, and concentrate on the sorts of activity you know make her feel comfortable. Try to help her to feel connected with family life, and its rhythms.**

depressed, but have recovered, let him know. He needs to know that depression is not necessarily a permanent state, and that he will feel better. He may feel that his despair will never lift, and that in turn will make him feel worse. He needs reassurance, but may be unable to ask for help, or even to articulate the way he feels.

Don't try to cope alone. Check out IDEA 52, *Waving or drowning?*, for tips on where to get help.

Try another idea...

You may want to suggest getting outside help, perhaps starting with a visit to your family doctor. Emphasise that any help the doctor offers can be refused if your teen does not want to accept it. A counsellor may also be able to help your teen, and your doctor may be able to suggest a suitable practitioner. If he refuses outside help, you can seek advice yourself and get ideas on how to deal with the situation. Look online for support groups – it will help him to know he is not alone. Make sure you notice any efforts your teen makes to deal with his problems, and be encouraging.

TAKE CARE OF YOURSELF

Parenting a teenager who is suffering depression can be stressful. Try to step back from the situation before you react, even when he acts strangely or in a way you find offensive. Ask for support – you do not have to cope alone. Ask close friends or relatives for help, or even to act as a sounding board. You need a safety valve. It may be worth asking someone your teen is very close to, such as a loved aunt or uncle, to help offer support.

Make sure you make time for yourself too. You need time away from the situation to replenish yourself. If you are to be able to help your teen, you need to take care of your own needs.

'If depression is creeping up and must be faced, learn something about the nature of the beast: you may escape without a mauling.'
DR R. W. SHEPHERD

Defining idea...

227

RISK OF SUICIDE

Be aware that some teenagers are at risk of suicide. Be alert to the warning signs, and seek immediate professional help from your doctor if you are worried about your teen. Seek help if your teenager:

- Is taking part in severe risk taking behaviour.
- Talking about or threatening suicide.
- Is experiencing a deep depressive episode that does not lift.
- Gives away personal possessions in bulk.
- Hints that he will not be a problem for much longer.

How did it go?

Q   Are some teenagers more likely to suffer from depression?

A   *Depression can affect anyone, but your teenager is more at risk if she has a close relative who has suffered from depression, or if she has recently experienced major stress such as prejudice, bereavement, feeling isolated or a break up.*

Q   My 18 year old seems to drink a lot of alcohol. Could this contribute to her depression?

A   *It could. She may be drinking to escape her problems but ironically, alcohol acts as a depressant and may make things worse. Alcohol can also interfere with your teen's ability to resolve any problems she has that are help-ing to cause her depression. If she is taking antidepressants, alcohol may interfere with their operation. Seek further information from http://www.about-teen-depression.com/*

Waving or drowning?

Recent research revealed that one in three parents feels like a failure.

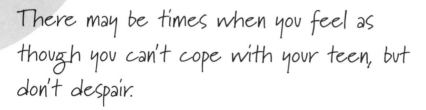
There may be times when you feel as though you can't cope with your teen, but don't despair.

You may have days when you just feel lost, and you don't know what to do with your teenager. You may even long for the days when she was little and hung on to your every word, almost feeling that you don't know the young person that lives in your house any more.

Relax – you are not alone. Most parents of teens have days like these, if they are honest. Knowing you are not alone can help you to bear the stress even if it does not solve the problem.

Like most parents, you may find that you search for reasons for her antisocial or unacceptable behaviour, turning amateur psychologist in an attempt to find an explanation. Don't waste your emotional energy on this. Whether you breastfed or not; whether your child was in full time nursery care virtually from birth or had a parent at home full time is all in the past. Let it stay there, and instead take stock of the here and now, and your present relationship with her. Don't waste time on self

Here's an
idea for
you... **If you are finding your teen unlovable, think about the time before the problems started. Use videos of family occasions, photos of birthday parties, holidays and trips as props. Hold on to the warm, loving feelings these memories awaken. When you look at your stroppy teenager, remember the child he once was and visualise the great adult he will one day be, and it will help you to cope with the difficulties of the 'here and now'.**

recrimination; it merely acts to erode the soul. Just because you are having difficulties, it does not mean you have been a bad parent; neither does it mean you teen is unable to change her behaviour. If your family life is constantly being disrupted by your teenager, it is only natural that you feel resentful towards her. You may feel that it is hard to love her – and feel guilty as a result. It is exhausting to try to balance family needs and work commitments, and a surly and out of control teenager can be the last straw.

If you are feeling overwhelmed, take time out to come up with a plan. Working constructively can help you to feel empowered, and lose your feelings of helplessness as you work out strategies to introduce change. Look at your relationship in general terms. There is no 'magic fix' for a rebellious teen; it is a long and difficult haul. The best parenting courses, books and advice can help – but the bottom line is the relationship you have with your teenager. The same nurturing, reasoning and adherence to the principles of right and wrong behaviour are needed now as when your teen was little.

You may feel that it is hard to treat her in a positive manner when she is being downright nasty – and that is only human. When you yourself are feeling hostile and hurt, acknowledge these feelings in yourself and recognise them as being a response to the situation. Then move on. If, in the hold of the spiral of helplessness you are feeling, you attempt to regain control by establishing lots of rules about everyday life instead of holding fast to a few important rules, you are bound to provoke resistance. Instead, be kind to yourself and do something that is all about you, and helps you to relax. A walk, reading, meeting friends – anything that reduces pressure in your life. Then attempt to engage again with your teen. Continue to invite her to take part in family life, and never give up. That does not mean allowing your teen to take advantage of you, and it may be tough. Reason with her, but make sure you tell her unequivocally what is acceptable behaviour – and what is not. Make sure there are consequences and sanctions for bad behaviour, which are always followed through. Firm boundaries provide stability for your teen, in a world where everything seems to be in a state of flux. Include your teen in setting the rules. It won't stop her breaking them from time to time, but it will help *you* to feel better if and when the rules are broken. A breach of rules is no longer an attack on your parental rules; it is a breach of family owned and created rules.

Make sure you do not try to control your teen by making personal attacks, or trying to induce guilt. This will only lead to more difficult behaviour. Instead, encourage independent thinking and the expression of feelings and ideas.

If you still feel overwhelmed, see a professional. See your family doctor and ask for a referral to a psychologist, or counsellor to talk about your concerns. Make sure you take care of yourself – and don't try to cope alone.

Feeling that you will never understand your teen? Read IDEA 7, *The still small voice: listening to your inner teenager*, to make that essential reconnection.

Try another idea...

'The wildest colts make the best horses.'
PLUTARCH

Defining idea...

231

How did it go?

Q **I feel as though I have completely lost control of my teenage son. I have always tried to treat him as an equal, but it's as if he is now the one with all the power. How can I cope?**

A *Whilst parents and children are equal as people, it is parents that wield the power. If you have lost control, your teen has in effect become the parent in your relationship. You need to once again become a strong force in his life, and set boundaries. Consider seeking some family counselling to help you get started.*

Q **I grounded my sixteen-year-old son recently, but he still kept going out. Any suggestions?**

A *It is difficult to 'make' a sixteen-year-old do anything. You need to sit down with him, and explain why you have rules – to keep him safe, and to care for the needs of the family as a whole. It is only through communication and negotiation that you will find a solution to this problem. Involve him in setting a system of simple rules, talking about consequences that will be invoked if he breaks them.*

Brilliant resources

GENERALLY USEFUL SITES

http://www.youthnoise.com/ (brilliant site for teens)
http://parentingteens.about.com/ (useful portal for many articles on parenting teens)
http://www.dr-bob.org/vpc/ (useful collection of 'virtual pamphlets' on health, welfare etc. for teens)
http://www.teenpuberty.com/ (general information site)
http://www.bbc.co.uk/teens/lads/ (wealth of information for teenage boys)
http://www.bbc.co.uk/teens/girls/ (wealth of information for teenage girls)
http://www.todaysparent.com/teen/index.jsp (useful parenting site)
http://www.teenwire.com (useful site for teens)
http://www.global-vision.org/teenager/ (online forum linking teens across the globe)
http://www.puberty101.com/ (information about puberty)
http://www.bygirlsforgirls.org/ (general site for girls and young women)
http://www.mysistahs.org/ (general site for girls and young women of colour)

GENERAL HEALTH, SEXUAL HEALTH AND REPRODUCTIVE ISSUES

http://www.teenhealthfx.com/ (health site for teens)
http://kidshealth.org/teen/ (comprehensive health site)
http://www.keepkidshealthy.com/adolescent/adolescentnutrition.html (advice on nutrition)
http://www.scarleteen.com/ (information about sexual health)
http://www.tht.org.uk/home/ (Terence Higgins Trust)
http://www.coolnurse.com/ (teen health site)
http://www.iwannaknow.org/ (teen sexual health)
http://womenshealth.about.com/cs/menstruation/a/firstperiodqate.htm (menarche Q&A)
http://kidshealth.org/teen/sexual_health/girls/menstrual_problems.html (coping with menstruation)
http://www.teenpregnancy.org/ (teenagers and pregnancy)

MENTAL AND EMOTIONAL HEALTH

http://familydoctor.org/590.xml (your teen's emotional health)
http://www.keepkidshealthy.com/adolescent/adolescentproblems/sleep.html (sleep problems)
http://www.aboutourkids.org/aboutour/articles/socially_anxious.html (anxiety)
http://www.aacap.org/about/glossary/index.htm (glossary of symptoms and mental illnesses)
http://www.nostigma.org/hope.html (mental health awareness)

DEPRESSION

http://www.psychologyinfo.com/depression/teens.htm (depression in teens)
http://www.clinical-depression.co.uk/Depression_Information/teen.htm (depression in teens)
http://www.teen-moods.net/ (teen depression support community)
http://www.about-teen-depression.com/ (help for teens with depression)

EATING DISORDERS

http://www.mirror-mirror.org/eatdis.htm (eating disorders)
http://www.youngwomenshealth.org/supportteens.html (for families of teens with eating disorders)
http://www.nationaleatingdisorders.org/ (eating disorders)

BULLYING AND SAFETY ISSUES

http://www.bullying.co.uk/ (bullying)
http://home.cybergrrl.com/dv/ (abuse and domestic violence advice)
http://www.safeyouth.org/scripts/teens.asp (personal safety)

LESBIAN, GAY, BISEXUAL AND TRANSGENDER TEENS

http://www.gayteens.org/ (website for LGBT teens)
http://www.pflag.org (for Parents, Families & Friends of LGBT people)
http://www.thetrevorproject.org/ (gay teens)
http://www.glsen.org (The Gay, Lesbian & Straight Education Network – building safe schools)

DRUGS AND ALCOHOL

http://www.teendrugabuse.us/teensandalcohol.html (drugs and alcohol)
http://www.al-anon.org/alateen.html (recovery program for young people)
http://www.alcoholics-anonymous.org/ (Alcoholics Anonymous)
http://www.factsontap.org/ (comprehensive information for college students)
http://www.freevibe.com/ (coping with peer pressure)
http://www.getoutraged.com/ (advice on smoking)
http://www.gottaquit.com/ (stopping smoking)
http://www.health.org/govpubs/phd688/ (teens helping friends)

LIVING WITH DENTAL BRACES

http://www.bda-dentistry.org.uk/smile/teens/index.cfm (all about braces)
http://www.bracesinfo.com/famous.html (famous people who have had braces)
http://www.familytlc.net/smiling_braces_pre.html (advice for parents)

BLENDED FAMILIES

http://www.thestepfamilylife.com (comprehensive site for blended families)
http://www.focusas.com/Stepfamily.html (stepfamilies and parenting after divorce)
http://teenagerstoday.com/resources/articles/stepfamilies.htm (helping teens adjust to stepfamilies)

EDUCATION

http://www.teenreads.com/ (great teen reading site)
http://www.education-otherwise.org/ (Education Otherwise homeschooling portal)
http://www.home-school.com/ (Home school world)
http://homeschooling.gomilpitas.com/ (Home's Cool website)
http://school.familyeducation.com/home-schooling/teen/37519.html (Homeschooling teens)
http://www.chrisdendy.com/ (ADHD website)
http://www.childrenfirst.nhs.uk/families/childdev/teenagers/stress.html (school stress)
http://parentingteens.about.com/od/collegeinfo/a/collegequestion_2.htm (thinking about college)

The end...

Or is it a new beginning?

We hope the ideas in this book will have inspired you to try some new ways to improve your relationship with your teenager. Perhaps we've given you some communication tips and insights into teen behaviour that have helped you realise that your child hasn't turned into a stranger (or a demon) and that with some adjustment, negotiation and understanding your family can all get on brilliantly.

So why not let us know all about it? Tell us how you got on. What did it for you – what really helped you feel more relaxed and happy around your teenagers? Maybe you've got some tips of your own you want to share (see next page if so). And if you liked this book you may find we have even more brilliant ideas that could change other areas of your life for the better.

You'll find the Infinite Ideas crew waiting for you online at www.infideas.com.

Or if you prefer to write, then send your letters to:
Raising teenagers
The Infinite Ideas Company Ltd
36 St Giles, Oxford, OX1 3LD, United Kingdom

We want to know what you think, because we're all working on making our lives better too. Give us your feedback and you could win a copy of another *52 Brilliant Ideas* book of your choice. Or maybe get a crack at writing your own.

Good luck. Be brilliant.

Offer one

CASH IN YOUR IDEAS

We hope you enjoy this book. We hope it inspires, amuses, educates and entertains you. But we don't assume that you're a novice, or that this is the first book that you've bought on the subject. You've got ideas of your own. Maybe our author has missed an idea that you use successfully. If so, why not put it in an email and send it to: yourauthormissedatrick@infideas.com, and if we like it we'll post it on our bulletin board. Better still, if your idea makes it into print we'll send you four books of your choice. or the cash equivalent. You'll be fully credited so that everyone knows you've had another Brilliant Idea.

Offer two

HOW COULD YOU REFUSE?

Amazing discounts on bulk quantities of Infinite Ideas books are available to corporations, professional associations and other organisations.

For details call us on:
+44 (0)1865 514888
fax: +44 (0)1865 514777
or e-mail: info@infideas.com

Where it's at ...

FREE book offer

Thank you for buying this book. We hope you enjoyed it and found lots of useful tips and have already been able to put them into practice. You can now improve another area of your life by taking advantage of our fabulous FREE book offer.* Does your relationship need some work or could you do with untangling that jungle you call your garden but aren't sure where to start? Perhaps you just want some tips on living a happier, healthier life. Once you've decided what you'd like to try, getting hold of your free book is simple. Look down the list below and decide which title you'd like to receive FREE of charge. Then either fill in the coupon and send it to the address below or call up and quote your unique offer code, giving the title of the book you would like to receive. Choose from the titles below:

☐ **Blooming pregnancy**
☐ **Create your dream garden**
☐ **Live longer**
☐ **Perfect parties**
☐ **Perfect weddings**

☐ **Re-energise your relationship**
☐ **Survive divorce**
☐ **Unleash your creativity**
☐ **Web sites that work**
☐ **Whole health**

How to place your order

Name: ....

Delivery address: ....

....

E-mail: ....

Telephone: ....

Unique offer code: RT1602

We never give details to third parties nor will we bombard you with lots of junk mail!

By post: Fill in all the relevant details, cut this page out (or photocopy it) and send it to: Infinite Ideas, 36 St Giles, Oxford OX1 3LD

Over the telephone: Call +44 (0) 1865 514 888. Please quote your unique offer code.

Any questions please call +44 (0) 1865 514 888 or e-mail info@infideas.com.

infiniteideas
www.52brilliantideas.com

For full details of these books and others in the **52 Brilliant Ideas** series please visit **www.52brilliantideas.com.**